WHO WAS SHAKESPEARE?

Operamania
Theatremania
The Wit of the Theatre
Who's Who in Shakespeare
A Companion to the Theatre

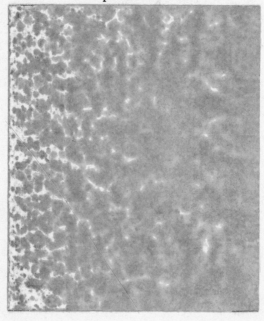

WHO WAS
Shakespeare?

The Man - The Times - The Works

ROBIN MAY

ST. MARTIN'S : NEW YORK

CONTENTS

LIST OF ILLUSTRATIONS

PLATES

7

List of Illustrations

To
my mother and father
who once
thought
that they had nurtured a
Shakespearean actor

PREFACE

This book is for serious students and casual Shakespeare-lovers alike. It is also, hopefully, for those who have been put off the plays at school or by unfortunate visits to the theatre. It ranges from Elizabethan London to the theories of the Baconians and others of that ilk, from the characters of Falstaff, Prince Hal and Hotspur to the state of traffic, human and mechanical, in Stratford, from the sources of the plays to the Royal Shakespeare Company, from Anne Hathaway's Cottage to Stratford, Ontario, and from Davenant's travesties of the plays to how Indians regard *Othello*.

Shakespeareans get so much joy from the plays that they sometimes fail to recognise or even admit the very real problems that beset others. For English-speaking audiences and students the main stumbling-block is some of the language. The conventions of verse, of female characters disguising themselves as men, can soon be absorbed by all but the most prosaic, but even those who know the plays well are likely to grasp only part of some lines and speeches. They get the essence, not the whole.

Some of the humour is too topical for modern audiences and some of it totally unfunny, condemning the actor to get his laughs by mugging, etc. As for the bawdy, which would be so much to modern taste, it is so obscure that only those who have learnt Eric Partridge's *Shakespeare's Bawdy* by heart can begin to keep up with it. To take a very simple case of punning. In Elizabethan times, 'nunnery' was sometimes used as a slang word for a brothel, which, if Shakespeare intended a pun, puts a very different complexion on Hamlet's command to Ophelia: 'Get thee to a nunnery'.

Another stumbling-block is Shakespeare as exam fodder, or indeed, as 'Eng Lit'. Good teachers can overcome this, and even less inspiring ones can set a class acting a play, or make sure that any chance of seeing it well acted will be seized. Fortunately, these methods are now generally accepted.

The good Shakespearean does not despise doing homework on the plays, any more than avid opera-goers neglect listening to records and reading libretti. However, this book is about the master entertainer of his own day and it aims to entertain, to add to the enjoyment of visits to Shakespearean productions, to prepare the reader for them, and to get the experienced Shakespeare-lover arguing for or against some of the opinions expressed. Discussing, arguing over, exulting in, railing against, and loving Shakespeare is a supreme way of tiring the sun with talking, and the moon too.

Non-English-speaking audiences, blessed though many of them are with good translations, can revel in Shakespeare's dramatic power, characters, thought and imagery, but they lose the incomparable verse. Yet, ironically, they often understand the plays better (given the right translation) than an average English-speaking audience, because the plays are given in the language they themselves use. Not that Shakespeare should ever be altered except on the very rarest occasions. Such an occasion happened at the very beginning of Peter Brook's career, when, in 1946, he was directing *King John* at Birmingham Rep. In the play is a great speech on 'Commodity', which now means 'expediency'– but how is the average member of an audience to know? So Peter Brook planted its meaning:

> That smooth-fac'd gentleman, *Expediency*,
> *Or, as they say*, tickling Commodity,
> Commodity, the bias of the world . . .

That was a legitimate addition, but generally speaking the reader or the audience should relax and revel in the entertainment. Homework helps, but it must always be an optional extra.

The short book list (p 137) contains many of the books that I have found stimulating in the past and helpful to me while writing this contribution to the ocean of Shakespeareana. Particularly useful were the two encyclopedias, while Ivor Brown's *Shakespeare* will always hold a special place in my affections because I first read it at a most impressionable time. I am grateful to the Cambridge University Press for allowing me to quote from *Shakespeare's Professional Skills* by Nevill Coghill, and I am indebted to Dr Levi Fox of the Shakespeare Birthplace Trust and the Shakespeare Centre for letting me use some of the Trust's photographs, and to Eileen Robinson and Robert Bearman for advice on which to select. J. C. Trewin was ready, as always, with good advice, and my wife encouraged me with cheering comments and constructive criticisms throughout.

R.M.

I

A SETTING FOR GENIUS

At length they all to merry London came. – Edmund Spenser

It is the duty of a genius to be born at the right moment, and no one has ever arranged things better than the greatest genius of all. Shakespeare's timing, 1564, was as incomparable as his art. If he had been born half a century or so earlier it is inconceivable that his fame would be a tenth of what it is, for the English language had not yet reached its age of eager, questing glory, there were few professional actors, no playhouses – the first was built in 1576 – and there was no blank verse.

This splendid and flexible form was invented by the Earl of Surrey to match the grandeur of Virgil's hexameters, and first appeared in print in his *Certain Bokes of Virgiles Aeneis* in 1557, a decade after he had been beheaded for trivial reasons, including ironically suggesting that his sister should become the king's mistress.

If Shakespeare had been young when Surrey was young, he would have been old in the high summer of the Elizabethan Age, the age of miracles of which his art was the supreme achievement. As it was, he may well have reached London, magic, volcanic Elizabethan London, in 1587, the year before the *annus mirabilis* itself when the Armada was defeated. London he was to call 'the quick forge and working-house of thought', 'quick' meaning vibrant with life.

Golden ages do not last long. Brightness soon falls from the air and the tarnish, which was there all the time, shows up more clearly than before. But Elizabeth I's England, the consolation of every English-speaking person with a spark of historical and artistic imagination, and the wonder of millions who know no English, was almost as extraordinary as its myth.

The Elizabethans inherited the Renaissance spirit late and made the most of it. They sometimes seem to have had gunpowder and champagne in their veins as well as blood. And they were ravished – a favourite word of theirs – by the world in which they delightedly found themselves.

Shakespeare's England was a time when a man could rise out of his class without any strain by sheer ability. He could hope to be spared poverty – though many were not – he could rejoice in music, song and poetry. A Mercutio – Renaissance man rampant – could be found in many parts of England and on the high seas, and not simply among the nobility.

Shakespeare's England was more truly musical than it has ever been since, with everyone expected at the very least to be able to take his or her part in a song, at best play an instrument. And with the language in sensuous and scintillating ferment, shot through with steely power and grandeur, and with its practitioners revelling in its flexibility, it is hardly surprising that poetry became a natural expression of life's joys and sorrows. It was accepted as something as delightfully commonplace as eating, drinking, loving and laughing.

This was the golden age of the true amateur, loving life, art and adventure. It was Sidney who was cited as 'the wonder of our age', but he was the star in a constellation. And above them all shone a vain, capricious, magnificent, clever woman, whose very signature shows her style and intelligence, Elizabeth, the impossible, glorious sovereign of the age of glory.

The doubters of today, forgetting that these men and women have not very much in common with mid-twentieth century city dwellers, bring up the other side of the glory, and they can be excused for it. Harmless old women lynched as witches; bear-baiting enjoyed by the very same people who revelled in Burbage's Hamlet; the obscene ritual of torture, of hanging, drawing and quartering. But these ancestors of today's English must be accepted and admired for what they were. Shakespeare, an affable, much-liked man, as his friends recorded, was part of this cruel world, where the plague added an extra, regular and terrible dimension of cruelty to life, and it is idle to delude ourselves that he was not part of it. The Victorians would not even allow him vigorous bawdy, assuming piously that it was 'by another hand'. For all his matchless humanity which, with his genius, ensures his pre-eminence and immortality, he was, like his contemporaries, that strange, glamorous creature, an Elizabethan.

London was the very heart of the Elizabethan world, though England was to remain an agricultural nation for more than two centuries. Shakespeare's plays are suffused with the country he knew as only a countryman can – and suffused with Warwickshire at that – but London, that swollen, stinking super-village of some quarter of a million people, made him too.

This was not simply because of the men and women he met there, who informed him even more than his books, as his writer's magpie-like mind picked up facts and ideas from everyone and everything. It was quite simply because London was the most exciting place on earth.

London! Evil-smelling, noisy, cramped, brawling, horrifying, glorious London, the stench of it – and Shakespeare was sensitive to smells – fighting with the aroma of fresh fields nearby. The Thames dominated the City, for it was the only good road, and on it some 2,000 boatmen in wherries and other small craft plied for trade, some of them over-charging their passengers shamelessly. Also on the river were the splendid barges of the Queen, the nobility and the great men of the city, and, crowning all, was London Bridge, much wider than today's, and a wonder of the Elizabethan world, with its huge houses, splendid array of shops, and shrunken traitors' heads stuck dramatically on poles as a deterrent. There were more of these grisly relics at Temple Bar.

Brutality was rampant, along with beauty. The theatre manager Henslowe and his star actor, Edward Alleyn, founder of Dulwich College, were made Masters of the Royal Game of Bears, Bulls and Mastiff dogs in 1594. Game? Not by today's reckoning. The Queen, her nobility, gentry and commons crossed the river to the South Bank, away from the jurisdiction of the City and its mainly pleasure-resenting Puritan rulers (who were rarely so sensitive about bloody sports as about the pleasure they gave). There, in a world of brothels, theatres, taverns and slums, was the Paris Garden.

In this arena, where the animals were latter-day gladiators, the excited throng watched a bear tied to a stake, the famous Harry Hunks, per-haps, his teeth shortened to prevent them being so lethal, but with his paws, claws and mighty grip unimpaired. His enemies were mastiffs, who fought him until some of them were killed. Then Hunks stood down and another bear went to the stake.

The second course set before the spectators was the sight of small boys whipping an old blind bear, while the third was a bull, tied, like the bears, to a stake, then attacked by mastiffs. So highly was the sport organised that men were on hand to catch the gored dogs, flung from the bull's horns, on a special frame. They were needed to fight again, to the vast delight of the Queen and her people, the very same patrons who were ravished by poetry, music, and the greatest drama ever written.

It is necessary to stress this (to us) strange appetite for feasting on pain as well as extreme beauty. Shakespeare was a man of his age though, without special pleading, it would seem that he was one of those who did not revel in such spectacles. It is fair to infer this from lines like Macbeth's:

> They have tied me to a stake; I cannot fly
> But bear-like I must fight the course.

Beauty and pain; the plague; the sonnet and the madrigal; the stench of the Fleet ditch; jordans emptied over passers-by; the only regular cleaners, scavenger kites; Harry Hunks bleeding to roars of joy, and other roars, born on the breeze from a theatre where Falstaff is delighting the groundlings and the great. We shall be visiting those theatres in the next chapter.

The riches of late Tudor London were stupendous. In Elizabeth's grandfather's reign a traveller noted fifty-two goldsmiths' shops in Cheapside, and now London was the leading city of Protestant Europe. In fine houses behind walls and gates, great businessmen did their work, many concluding deals in the magnificent Royal Exchange, the country's first shopping precinct, built by Gresham in 1566. Patriot buccaneers like Drake and Hawkins served them well, and their instinct for, and skill in, trade ranged continents and oceans. When western Europe was cut off from them they made the world their market. Like Antonio they could find that their argosies were 'richly come to harbour suddenly'.

The nobility, as keen as everyone on making their fortunes overseas, had moved their London homes from the City to palaces along the

Strand and beyond. Neither they nor the Queen had a stronghold in the City, which was a state within a state to be wooed and handled with care. Royal and aristocratic power lay at Westminster, Whitehall and the Tower, though the Commons at Westminster needed wooing too, as Gloriana knew so well.

Into this seething, splendid, barbaric, cultured city young William Shakespeare rode or walked at some unknown date in the late 1580s. There he enjoyed some fame and much popularity, and was liked and admired as a man – 'of right happy and copious industry', as John Webster put it. Though some glimpsed that he was 'for all time', it was left to later generations to realise his supreme genius, and to a lucky, unguessable number in each of those generations to love him more than any man that ever lived.

2

THE MAN

Why, here's our fellow Shakespeare puts them all down. – Anon, *Return from Parnassus* (1601)

'Gulielmus filius Johannes Shakspere' was christened at the Church of the Holy Trinity in Stratford-upon-Avon on 26 April 1564, one of a miserly number of facts that we know about the greatest of Englishmen. We are lucky, in fact, to have so many, for of the other Elizabethan and Jacobean dramatists only Jonson is better documented, partly because he lived longer.

Fortunately, thanks to awe-inspiring research in our century by historians and literary men, an extraordinary amount has been discovered about the Stratford of his day, and also about his environment and circle of acquaintances in London. However, biographers are still faced with gaps in his story so vast that they have to fall back on guesses that they hope are inspired, whereas a single biographical chapter can stick firmly to facts, reasonable deductions and likely gossip.

Shakespeare's birthday may not have been St George's Day, 23 April, but it probably was, for christenings were performed as soon as possible after birth. John and Mary Shakespeare would have followed custom for they had already lost two children in infancy, named Joan and Margaret.

There are over eighty ways of spelling the family's name, for Elizabethan spelling was delightfully haphazard enough to make a modern child – or grown-up – sick with envy. 'Shakespeare' was William's most usual version in print, though of his own six known signatures only two tally, and none of them are spelt as we know the name. He probably pronounced his name with a short 'a' as in 'shack'.

Both his parents were Midlanders. Baconians and others who doubt that he wrote his own plays often portray Shakespeare and his family as at the bottom of the social heap (preferably a dunghill), having fatally failed to hear about the knowledge of the family gathered in the last seventy or so years. Their case rests on grossest snobbery as well as ignorance. In fact, John, in 1564, was a successful glover and wool-dealer of Stratford, which was already an important small town of some 2,000 people. His wife Mary was one of the eight daughters of Robert Arden, a prosperous yeoman farmer of Wilmcote near Stratford.

John was a leading member of his community in 1564, having already served in various posts, including Chamberlain. In 1569 he became Bailiff, the town's leading citizen. He signed documents with a cross and, having been brought up at Snitterfield, where there was no school, he may or may not have been able to write: many businessmen could not at that time. But the sign of the cross was common enough as the equivalent of an oath in medieval times and was still used in the country, even sometimes by those who could write, so there is no proof of his literacy or lack of it.

Part of his job was to dress the white skins of sheep, goats and deer and he would help kill the animals, which may account for that gossip John Aubrey's being told that Shakespeare's father was a butcher. Born ten years after Shakespeare's death, he heard how young Will killed a calf in 'high style' and would make a speech while doing the job. 'Nothing improbable in that,' as A. L. Rowse has written, and it is a pleasant thought. References to skins are plentiful in the plays.

John probably married Mary, complete with an inheritance, in 1557. They had eight children in all (see the family tree on p 22), including Gilbert who became a haberdasher, Joan who married a hatter named Hart, and Edmund who became an actor. The Harts' son became owner of the birthplace and workplace – the assumed birthplace – in Henley Street. But more of this in Chapter 6.

No records of pupils of the grammar school in Shakespeare's day exist, but William, as the son of a leading citizen, obviously went there, the grammar in question being Latin, day after day after day, Lily's *Latin Grammar* to be exact. Entrance was at seven, after a little elementary education in letters, numbers and religion. 'Small Latin and less Greek' Jonson was later to say that his friend possessed. His small Latin included a passion for Ovid, who was adored by most of the Elizabethan poets and used by Shakespeare for subject-matter, charac-

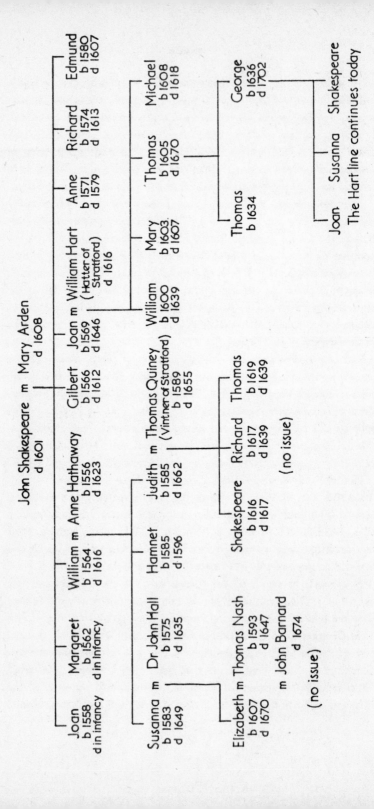

John Shakespeare m Mary Arden
d 1601   d 1608

Joan
b 1558
d in infancy

Margaret
b 1562
d in infancy

William m Anne Hathaway
b 1564   b 1556
d 1616   d 1623

Gilbert
b 1566
d 1612

Joan m William Hart
b 1569   (Hatter of
d 1646   Stratford)
          d 1616

Anne
b 1571
d 1579

Richard
b 1574
d 1613

Edmund
b 1580
d 1607

Susanna m Dr John Hall
b 1583   b 1575
d 1649   d 1635

Hamnet
b 1585
d 1596

Judith m Thomas Quiney
b 1585   (Vintner of Stratford)
d 1662   b 1589
           d 1655

William
b 1600
d 1639

Mary
b 1603
d 1607

Thomas
b 1605
d 1670

Michael
b 1608
d 1618

Elizabeth m Thomas Nash
b 1607   b 1593
d 1670   d 1647

m John Barnard
d 1674

(no issue)

Shakespeare
b 1616
d 1617

Richard
b 1617
d 1639

Thomas
b 1619
d 1639

(no issue)

Thomas
b 1634

George
b 1636
d 1702

Joan.   Susanna   Shakespeare
The Hart line continues today

ters and even phrases, the *Metamorphoses* being his treasure trove. *Venus and Adonis*, Pyramus and Thisbe and the statue scene in *The Winter's Tale* are among the proofs of this.

The world's greatest historical dramatist had little chance to learn any history at school. His inspired plundering of Holinshed's *Chronicles* and North's *Plutarch* occurred when he was a man. But along with Ovid there were two other sources of inspiration which came in childhood, the Bible and the Prayer Book. Attendance at church in a country town was obligatory, but even so his familiarity with both is remarkable, no less than forty books inspiring allusions.

Yet Shakespeare's religion remains a mystery – which has not stopped both Catholics and Protestants claiming him as their own. To complicate matters, government censorship cut down religious argument in plays, and the situation in Stratford confuses us further because, like many another English town at the time, advocates of the old and new religion were present. So were supporters of the dismal third creed that was Puritanism.

It is probable that John Shakespeare was a Catholic. After he had fallen into financial difficulties in 1577 and had to part with property, he slipped out of public life and was later fined £40, a very large sum, possibly because he went to Catholic services and not the parish church. He regularly failed to attend around 1592, though the law required it. His will, too, suggests Catholicism. He died in 1601, his fortunes having been restored several years before, doubtless by his son.

But William? His Tudor Establishment outlook would seem to make him an upholder, if not a fervent one, of the Church of England. He can hardly have been a Puritan (though his son-in-law, Dr Hall, was one), not least because the Puritans were so fervently hostile to his dual professions, actor and playwright. So let us leave him as a conforming Anglican, at Stratford at least. When sexual desire, frustration and bitterness were tormenting him in London it is hard to believe that religion often entered his head.

Scholars and theologians meanwhile argue over verbal clues, forgetting that Shakespeare, the ultimate Renaissance Man in his art at least, was all things to all his characters, the supreme example of divine neutrality of attitude, even though in a line of parts from Berowne, through Mercutio, the Bastard in *King John*, Hotspur and Falstaff to Hamlet and a few more, we seem to get close to the feelings of the real man. (In his *Shakespeare*, John Middleton Murry called this line of parts the Shakespeare Man.)

After school, possibly because of his father's troubles, and to help in the shop, he did not go to a university. Few great playwrights have. Given the mystery of genius, his education had been sufficient, as was that of Dickens, another non-intellectual popular genius. Academic training cannot produce the ultimate gift of word mastery, nor can it train a writer to be a snapper-up of unconsidered trifles, which every great and not-so-great creative author must be. Shakespeare drank in Warwickshire, its people, its sounds, the seasonal sights of its countryside, and richly reproduced them all in his plays. When he came to London, he only had to read widely, keep his eyes and ears open in taverns, in Court when he acted there, and with his friends of every class, travellers included, to absorb all the knowledge he needed for his plays. Given the mystery of genius.

As certain as his schooling were his visits to the touring companies of players at the Guild Hall. His very first may have been as early as 1569, when the Queen's Interluders played at Stratford, giving their first performance to his father, as Bailiff, and other leading citizens. It was the Bailiff's duty to check a show for its political and religious contents.

In his boyhood, the Earl of Worcester's Men, Leicester's Men and Warwick's Men were only some of the visitors, and there were also pageants and folk plays to be enjoyed, as well as wandering clowns, tumblers and musicians. So he had the luck to be exposed to theatre from infancy.

The first hard facts in Shakespeare's life since his christening are far more confusing than most traditions about him. On 27 November 1582, an entry was made in the Bishop of Worcester's register granting a marriage licence, with only one asking of banns, between William Shakespeare and Anne Whateley of Temple Grafton, a village near Stratford. The very next day a bond of £40 is recorded in another entry. It was given by two farmers of Stratford, Fulk Sandells and John Richardson, exempting the Bishop from all liability if the marriage of 'William Shagspere' and 'Anne Hathway' of Stratford should prove unlawful.

These sensational adjacent entries have legitimately given the green light to romantics and cynics alike. For want of better, the most likely explanation is that the clerk who made the entry which has caused such a stir made a mistake. He is known to have been error-prone and to have had a William Whateley on his mind because of a legal dispute. As for Temple Grafton, it was five miles from Stratford and the local gossips, and was where the wedding no doubt took place, probably on 30 November or 1 December. There are no records of Whateleys at Temple Grafton, and the single banns and the urgency were due to Anne's pregnancy. There are, of course, more romantic and village Don Juanish explanations.

Anne was eight years older than her husband. Her rightly loved house was actually her father Richard's, a prosperous farmer of Shottery, once detached from, but now on the outskirts of, Stratford.

Much 'evidence' has been found in the plays to support the view that the marriage was not a happy one, and the notorious 'second best bed' of the will has been taken by some to be an insult. Yet in fact we know nothing of the marriage, which may have been tolerable or even happy. The sonnets, the only place where Shakespeare the man clearly reveals himself, proclaim him unfaithful, just as the plays reveal a highly sexed side to him, but beyond these justifiable assumptions all is guesswork.

'Let still the woman take An elder than herself', advises Orsino in *Twelfth Night*, which hardly proves that Shakespeare was talking about his own marriage, though 'War is no strife To the dark house and the detested wife' in *All's Well* is a terrible statement: make war rather than a bad marriage! But what does it prove? The aftermath of a quarrel, or merely the poet's artistry?

Anne died in 1623 and, according to Mr Dowdall, who got it from an ancient clerk in 1693, she earnestly desired to be laid in the same grave as her William. He certainly returned to her regularly, or was it to Stratford? As for the bed, she may have got the best one by right, or it may have gone to the Halls. She may have even liked the second best bed!

Shakespeare was passionately interested in women, and in one woman in particular, but Shakespeare, the gentleman of Stratford, had a wife who was part of his life there. 'I surmise that Anne was William's "steady",' wrote Ivor Brown very sensibly. But, barring a sudden find, we shall never know for certain.

Their firstborn was Susanna, baptised on 26 May 1583, six months after the wedding. On 2 February 1585, twins were baptised, Hamnet and Judith. These two events are the only indisputable facts known about Shakespeare between his marriage and the attack made on him by the dying Robert Greene in 1592, except for a passing mention of him in 1588. This was in a Bill of Complaint which his parents and he brought against one John Lambert over property, but it does not prove he was still in Stratford.

The most popular choice for his year of departure is 1587, a year no less than five acting companies visited Stratford, and when a school-friend named Richard Field took over a printer's business in London having married the owner's widow. But what he had been doing before he left, what, indeed, he was doing until 1592, is a mystery dark enough to allow all sorts of theories, many based on the old nonsense that a writer has to experience a thing to write about it.

So we have Shakespeare the sailor, the soldier, the traveller, the school-master and the lawyer, the wildest conjectures being by William Bliss in *The Real Shakespeare*, who has our William as a boy sailing with Drake round the world and later being shipwrecked on the Adriatic coast – 'This is Illyria, lady' – returning via Italy and France.

Brushing aside the sheer unlikelihood of the Drake story, it must be admitted that Shakespeare's writing on shipwrecks in *The Tempest* and *Pericles* was very vivid, but then so is his description via Hotspur of the popinjay of a staff officer who appeared on the battlefield of Holmedon. Internal evidence does suggest, however, that he may have been a tutor and also that he worked for a time in a lawyer's office. (Professor Nicholas Wright of Wesleyan University, Connecticut, has recently claimed himself ready to prove that Shakespeare was a solicitor's clerk in Westminster after leaving Stratford. All except Baconians will wish the professor success.)

Aubrey heard from Beeston, son of a colleague of Shakespeare's, that he had been 'a School-master in the Countrey'. More probably he was a tutor and the place may have been Gloucestershire because of references in *Richard II* and in the magical Shallow scenes in *Henry IV Part 2*. As for the law, legal jargon abounds, not least in a speech over a skull in *Hamlet* which overflows with it and, as Anthony Burgess has observed, is quite irrelevant.

Annoyingly, because it wrecks his assumed boyhood, it is just possible that he was the William Shakeshafte 'nowe dwellynge' with Alexander Houghton of Lea in Lancashire in 1581, who commended him to Sir Thomas Hesketh of Rufford. Hesketh had his own actors in 1587 and Shakespeare could have been a tutor and actor with him, using a variation of his grandfather's name. An unlikely twist.

However, he must be got to London, so let us side with those who have him joining the Queen's Men at Stratford in 1587, or arranging to join them that winter in London. As Aubrey heard, he was a 'handsome well shap't man'. He was clearly ambitious and, as we know, was very likeable. He would be near enough home if there was a family crisis and we can only wonder if his decision to go to London provoked a monumental one with Anne. Whatever happened, on an unknown day he crossed Clopton Bridge, as millions have done since, and set off to restore the family's fortune.

Some believe that he set off at a gallop, having been caught poaching on Sir Thomas Lucy's fine estate at Charlecote. The Puritan knight had no deer park, but there were plenty of deer nearby, and the tradition is a seventeenth-century one. Sir Thomas was an ardent conservationist and had to contend with the fact that deer poaching was a popular sport with all classes. Shakespeare may well be getting his own back in the very first scene of *The Merry Wives*, if Shallow is Lucy. There are plenty of references to hunting in the plays and poems, Shakespeare sympathising with the 'poor frightened deer' and characterising the hounds as 'coward dogs'. Remembering 'fawning spaniels', one can safely say that he was no dog-lover.

However, even if he did fall foul of Sir Thomas, there is no evidence that it caused his departure from Stratford: he could have been caught at the game earlier. Or the whole story may be myth.

He reached London at the time of Marlowe's *Tamburlaine the Great*, the most influential event in the history of English drama. Before substantiating such a statement, which is neither daring nor original, it is necessary to examine the heady, expanding theatre of the day, which, like the English language itself, was in thrilling ferment.

The greatest theatre depends on the trinity of great drama, great acting and great audiences. In its supreme form, the drama is always new, and only twice in history has this happened, in nineteenth-century

Italy, when a whole people become opera-crazed, and in Elizabethan and Jacobean England, especially in London.

The truth of the trinity holds good even today, the age of the star director and ensemble (which last was surely a feature of Shakespeare's company as well). As the superb Royal Shakespeare Company has sometimes found to its cost, the very greatest plays – Shakespeare's tragedies and a handful of others – must have star players who can aspire to greatness in the supreme roles, or they suffer at the heart. At the heart of Marlowe was Edward Alleyn, at the heart of Shakespeare was Richard Burbage.

Drama, the first of the trinity, died in Britain in the Dark Ages, being re-born in England in the churches in Norman times. By 1300, church dramas, the Bible histories known as Miracles and Mysteries, had reached the market-places and were being performed by the guilds, the story of Jonah by the fishmongers, Noah by the shipwrights, and so on. The pattern was the same on the Continent.

The Moralities, complete with personified virtues, followed, the most famous being *Everyman*, which was probably first written in Dutch around 1495. By the time Elizabeth came to the throne, however, there was still no evidence of the trinity. When it came, events were to move even more rapidly than they did in a not entirely dissimilar situation – the growth of the cinema industry in Hollywood from around 1910.

The key early Elizabethan plays were not acted by professionals. *Ralph Roister Doister*, the first English Renaissance comedy, was written by a schoolmaster named Udall for his pupils, while the Renaissance tragedy, *Gorboduc*, was written by students of the Inner Temple and performed by their friends before the Queen in 1561. *Gammer Girton's Needle*, which peopled a stage with mere English, as the Queen once boasted she was, was given at Cambridge.

The dominant force on the stage until the 1580s was companies of boy actors. The children of the Royal Chapel and of St Paul's were near-professionals even though they did not act in the public theatres. Shakespeare had a dig at these 'little eyases, that cry out on the top of question and are most tyrannically clapp'd for it' in *Hamlet*.

Professional actors 'strolled' during the fifteenth century. Ironically, in view of what the Tudors and Shakespeare did to him, an early patron of the drama was Richard Crookback. These early players gave 'Interludes', which were usually small-scale farces and edifying moral tales and were sometimes performed literally by three men and a boy. John Heywood was the best-known writer of them, his work being given at Court, but mostly they were the bread and butter of the strolling players.

In Elizabethan times a man without a craft was classed as a vagabond, and actors escaped the whip only if they were 'servants' of a nobleman or rich gentleman. They were expected to perform for their patron only on special or festive occasions. The rest of the time they acted in market-places and inn yards and halls for a living.

The Earl of Leicester's Men were the best-known band of players for much of Elizabeth's reign, and it was they who first occupied the Theatre in 1576. This first English playhouse was a natural develop-ment, for it was inspired by the inn yards in which the players had raised their platforms to perform, and which they would continue to use. There is only one drawing of an Elizabethan theatre, which shows the interior of the Swan Theatre. It is only a copy, for the original, done by Johannes de Witt, a Dutch student on a visit to London in the 1590s, was lost. Fortunately, a friend of his had made a copy, repro-duced on p 30. Its accuracy has been disputed, but at least it exists, the foundation stone of an entire Shakespearean industry.

The popularity of the professionals dates from the erection of the Theatre, built by James Burbage, one of Leicester's Men, whose brother-in-law put up the money. He was later to convert part of Blackfriars priory into the famous private theatre. This was in 1596, two decades after his first incomparable gift to English drama. His elder son Cuthbert was a theatre manager, his younger, Richard, a great actor, and the luckiest of them all, because he was the first to play Richard III, Hamlet, Lear, Othello and other unparalleled creations.

The Theatre was outside the City limits, as were later ones, including the Curtain (1576), the Rose (1587), the Swan (1595) and the Globe (1599). The Theatre was built in the 'liberty' of Hollywell, Shoreditch, by Finsbury Fields, and the Curtain not far from it. The other three mentioned were on the South Bank, also in liberties, ie free from the City. This was sheer necessity, more so every year as the theatres boomed. Hostility to them, the actors and the audiences grew rapidly, the reasons being religious, medical and economic.

tectum

porticus

orchestra

mimorum
ædes

proscænium

planities siue arena

huntum sed dispari et structura, bestiarium comitte-
oni destinatum, in quo multi ursi, tauri, et stupenda
magnitudinis canes, distructis cantis et septis aluntur; qu

So fierce did this hostility become in London that the stage was saved only by royal and, especially, aristocratic patronage and protection. At least the health objection was understandable, and in plague years the actors vanished on tour when deaths in the capital rose above a fixed limit. And employers could reasonably object to the vast number of apprentices who, along with tradesmen of every sort, spent their afternoons at the play. As many as one in eight Londoners may have been *regular* playgoers, a ratio never equalled since.

But the most notorious objections were religious, with Protestant extremists leading the attack. Historians object to the word, as being too vague, but it is convenient to join the majority and call the extremists Puritans.

They were thick in the City, the preachers being naturally the most vocal. Soon after the first playhouse opened, a holy man gave the lead that others were to follow:

> Behold the sumptuous theatre houses, a continual monument of London's prodigality and folly . . . The cause of plagues is sin, if you look to it well; and the cause of sin are plays; therefore the cause of plagues are plays.

Inside the houses of Satan the groundlings ('stinkards') stood in the yard with the sky above them, and gazed at the stage, forty feet or so square. They paid a penny, while the top price, probably for a boxed-off lords' room on the lower gallery, was a shilling.

The theatres were round or polygonal, after which un-bold statement guesswork and fierce arguments begin. Only the Fortune is well-documented because its contract survives. Built in 1600 by Alleyn and his new partner, the manager Philip Henslowe, it was to be like the Globe, but square, 80 feet outside and 55 feet inside. It had three galleries, four partitioned-off gentlemen's rooms and a number of twopenny rooms. The stage was 43 feet broad and extended $27\frac{1}{2}$ feet to the middle of the yard. When it was rebuilt after a fire which gutted it in 1621, it became a round brick building.

The insides of the theatres were handsomely painted. The first Globe was thatched, the cause of its destruction in 1613, when, at the première of *Henry VIII*, a gunshot set the thatch on fire while 'King Henry [was] making a masque at the Cardinal Wolsey's house', as Sir Henry Wootton wrote in a letter. The 'idle smoke' rapidly kindled into fire which 'ran round like a train' and destroyed everything within an hour. '. . . one man had his breeches set on fire, that would perhaps have broiled him, if he had not by the benefit of a provident wit put it out with the bottle ale'. It was rebuilt in a year, only to be pulled down by Puritan edict in 1644.

The stage, perhaps 5 feet high, was equipped with trapdoors, while entrances and exits were made through doors upstage right and left. Between the doors there was (unless Dr Leslie Hotson is right) an inner stage, probably curtained off, which was used for bedrooms, prisons or 'discoveries' like the moment when Prospero sees Ferdinand and Miranda playing chess in his cell. Behind the inner stage was the tiring house (dressing-room), and above was an upper stage which could serve as battlements (*Richard II*) or a balcony (*Romeo and Juliet*).

Though all that *matters* is the stage thrusting out into the yard, and that there were doors and an upper stage, it must be mentioned that Dr Hotson places the tiring house under the stage and does not believe in the existence of an inner stage. For him, the Globe was theatre-in-the-round.

A few favoured spectators appear to have been allowed to sit on the sides of the stage of some theatres, a custom not finally broken until Garrick's day. The roof which projected over the stage was supported by two pillars. It was usually known as 'the heavens'. 'Hell' was below the stage, a reminder of the old Mystery and Miracle plays, where a trap was Hell's Mouth. From the heavens, and via a trap door, machinery could let down special effects or scenery, while somewhere above the stage was a musicians' gallery. At the very top was a turret where a flag flew on performance days. The start was announced by three blasts of a trumpet at 2pm, probably later in the private indoor theatres which we will come to in their Shakespearean context, and the plays were probably acted without an interval.

Scenery was basic – as it is again today – a tree serving for a forest, benches and a table for an inn, plus plenty of descriptive writing. Could the 'cockpit' of the Globe 'hold The vasty fields of France'? Could the groundlings see the horses 'Printing their proud hoofs i' the receiving earth'? Being word-drunk Elizabethans, for whom poetry was heightened living, there can have been no problem, especially in the company of Burbage and his colleagues.

Page 33 (above) Clopton Bridge, Stratford-upon-Avon, from *Picturesque views of the Warwickshire Avon* by Samuel Ireland, 1795; (below) the kitchen of Shakespeare's Birthplace

Page 34 (above) The schoolroom of King Edward VI School, Stratford-upon-Avon, which Shakespeare must have attended; (below) doggerel on Shakespeare's tomb in Holy Trinity Church, Stratford-upon-Avon

GOOD FREND FOR IESVS SAKE FORBEARE,
TO DIGG THE DVST ENCLOASED HARE.
BLESE BE Y MAN Y SPARES THES STONE
AND CVRST BE HE Y MOVES MY BONE

But constumes were often fine, and plenty of properties were used. Though plays were given in modern dress, some suggestion of antiquity was allowed, a plumed helmet for a Roman, and so on. Colours had meanings, willow-green for the lovelorn, blood-red for the mighty and valiant.

Today, we have returned to the speed of action of Shakespeare's time, so essential especially in plays which range England, like *Henry IV*, and the ancient world, like *Antony and Cleopatra*. The tyranny of acres of scenery, at its most inflated worst in the 1850s in Charles Kean's productions, is finally over, even if ugliness now sometimes reigns in its stead. The first major reformer, following earlier pioneers, was William Poel who, in the age of Beerbohm Tree and live rabbits on stage, returned to Elizabethan simplicity.

The boy actors who played women's parts, not to be confused with those in the boys' companies, had a strict apprenticeship within a company, and the quality of the best of them is proved by the trust that Shakespeare had in them. He could not allow kisses to be rained on them, but his audience did not expect it. So it comes about that *Antony and Cleopatra* is, as Granville Barker noted, 'a tragedy of sex without one single scene of sexual appeal'. Yet where in all drama is there a tragedy of love to compare with it? And what of the daring with which Shakespeare entrusted a boy Cleopatra with the breath-taking dramatic irony of:

> I shall see
> Some squeaking Cleopatra boy my greatness
> I' the posture of a whore.

Legend once insisted that the audiences at the Globe, and at the other public playhouses, were a rabble of nut-cracking, orange-eating, foul-smelling simpletons, leavened by a handful of intelligent nobles, and livened up by prostitutes and cut-purses. They may have smelt foul. Shakespeare was one of those who noticed. How few moderns would keep fragrant without a decent water supply? But how did the greatest of all theatre audiences, the third pillar of the trinity, get its other reputations?

Mainly through the attacks of the many enemies of the stage, especially preachers, but partly through soured playwrights. This unique audience is beyond sociological research, though we know it included all classes,

C

even if the actual percentage of genuine members of the proletariat cannot be guessed. The groundlings, contrary to their myth, included not only the lowest classes, but craftsmen, shopkeepers and their wives, respectable women, as foreign visitors noted. Of course, the criminals were there, perhaps enjoying the play between snatches, and so were the racier ladies. As Dekker helpfully observed: 'By sitting on the stage, if you be a Knight, you may happily get yourself a Mistresse: if a mere Fleet Street Gentleman, a wife.'

This audience of all classes – a unique phenomenon in Britain for great art – wept with abandon. This happy custom lasted over 200 years, after which public displays of emotion anywhere became more and more suspect – to the extent that tears from Winston Churchill could be thought worthy of press comment.

The Elizabethan wonder audience also voiced its disapproval with great spirit, hence some of the acid remarks about it. But its silence was total when heart and mind were gripped. After Jonson was dead, Leonard Digges recalled in verse how Shakespeare captured his audiences in a way that his friend and rival did not. It appeared as a prefix to a 1640 edition of the poems.

> oh how the Audience
> Were ravish'd, with what wonder they went hence,
> When some new day they would not brooke a line,
> of tedious (though well laboured) *Catilines*;
> . . . when let but *Falstaffe* come,
> *Hall*, *Poines*, the rest you scarce shall have a roome
> All is so pestered: let but *Beatrice*
> And *Benedicke* be seene, loe in a trice
> The Cockpit Galleries, Boxes, all are full
> To heare *Maluoglio* that crosse garter'd Gull.

This tribute is not simply useful as an indication of the popularity of certain plays – to which we will return – but as a glimpse of that marvel of an audience. As Shakespeare developed from the basic, but potent, stark simplicities of *Henry VI Part 1* and *Titus Andronicus*, it is reasonable to suppose that he sometimes 'lost' some of his auditors, though there is little proof that he did. Dekker suggests that such moments occurred, but the way he words his comment is exciting and significant:

                    on tip-toe to reach up
    And (from rare silence) clap their brawny hands
    T' applaud what their charmed soul scarce understands.

'Rare' should be understood as in 'O rare Ben Jonson'.

Today, the nearest equivalent to these ravished audiences can be found at the opera, the ballet and the Proms. Cheers are rarely heard in a theatre except on some first night, and even then, since Irving's day, few actors have brought down the house in the old volcanic way, except, on occasion, Olivier. Their excellence is not in question, and their audiences are often gripped and breathless with panic exaltation. But loudly expressed emotion, as Shakespeare, Kean and Irving knew it, is left to followers of music and the dance.

Audiences at the public theatres were perhaps some 2,000 or so, though de Witt estimated the Swan's total as 3,000. By the mid-1580s they were ready for great drama, and when they got it the trinity came into being. Each part of it spurred the other on to new heights.

Christopher Marlowe, the Canterbury shoemaker's son, sealed the trinity and, in doing so, set the theatre on fire. Born the same year as Shakespeare, he lacked his humanity and humour, yet, as Swinburne wrote of him,

> He is the greatest discoverer, the most daring and inspired pioneer, in all our poetic literature. Before him there was neither genuine blank verse nor a genuine tragedy in our language. After his arrival the way was prepared, the paths were made straight, for Shakespeare.

This shadowy genius, who created titans, transformed blank verse into his own brazen, beautiful, often stupendous 'mighty line'. And he transfigured the base metal of his predecessors into true tragedy. Swinburne rightly paints him as a John the Baptist. Shakespeare was to tease Marlowe and his actors with Pistol and his overblown verse, but he clearly loved his only true rival's art, the man he called 'Dead shepherd'. Marlowe, killed in a tavern brawl in 1593, could never have written Shakespeare – the eccentrics who believe that (undead) he did so simply do not know their own hero – but he must have inspired him profoundly. In our own time, we have seen how *Look Back in Anger* inspired a generation of young writers to turn to drama as a means of expression, and it needs little imagination to conjure up the effect that *Tamburlaine* had on Shakespeare the first time he heard and saw it.

It was the Admiral's Men who gave Marlowe's plays. Edward Alleyn was their star, and England's first great actor, worthy to play Tamburlaine, Faustus and Barabas. Whether or not Shakespeare was criticising Alleyn's acting in Hamlet's advice to the Players, as some believe, there is every reason to think that Burbage was a greater actor and, as befitted the parts he acted, a more subtle artist. Yet fortunate the age which had two such stars to act in the plays of two such unmatchable talents.

The talent of the slower starter was in evidence by 1592, as we shall see, but before that we have only late tradition to help us. Shakespeare, according to his first biographer, Nicholas Rowe (1709), began, reasonably enough, in 'a very mean Rank'. Rowe got many of his facts from the great Restoration actor, Thomas Betterton, who had, in turn, collected them from Stratford, from theatrical tradition, and from Sir William Davenant.

Davenant liked people to believe that he was Shakespeare's son, which was not impossible. Shakespeare 'was wont to go to his native country once a year' (Aubrey) and is reputed to have broken off his journeys at Oxford, staying with Davenant's parents, a vintner and his wife. And certainly, whether the boy was a son, a godson, or no relation, he was to become a brilliant all-rounder – dramatist, soldier, theatre manager, Poet Laureate – even if he did try to 'improve' Shakespeare's plays. *Macbeth* was given dancing, singing, flying witches. More of such atrocities are related in Chapter 4.

Shakespeare probably began in the theatre in the 'mean Rank' of hired man, in which company we do not know. Hired men might be stage hands, prompters, small part actors, gatherers or wardrobe assistants, their wages being 6 shillings a week. The legend that Shakespeare's very first job in London was organising a group of boys to hold gentlemen's horses outside the theatre is also reasonable enough, for as a family man he had to make money at once. When he started in the theatre, his evident talent must have got him on fast, and so must the well-documented fact that he was much liked. As to his acting ability, the parts he is reputed to have played – old Adam in *As You Like It*, the Ghost in *Hamlet*, etc – do not necessarily prove that he was confined to old character roles and 'heavies' while still young, though he may have had weight and maturity beyond his years. It is probable that his colleagues wanted him to keep writing and did their best to confine him to smaller parts. He doubtless directed his own plays, and, though we can never know just what Elizabethan acting was like – how formal, how realistic – he must have been a superb director, if his instructions via Hamlet to the Players are typical of his rehearsal methods.

In March 1592, *Harey the vj* was first given by Strange's Men, which may well have been Shakespeare's company, for it was to become the Lord Chamberlain's Men, with him in it, two years later. The play was very probably his *Henry VI Part 1*, and that September, the envious, bitter, dying Robert Greene attacked him in Groatsworth of Wit, while railing against players in general:

> Yes trust them not: for there is an upstart Crow, beautified with our feathers, that with his *Tygers hart wrapped in a players hyde* [a clear allusion to a famous line in *Henry VI Part 3*] supposes he is as well able to bombast out a blanke verse as the best of you: and being an absolute *Iohannes fac totum*, is in his own conceit the onely Shake-scene in a countrey.

Fame indeed! The publisher of the tract, Henry Chettle, apologised most handsomely in print, but we are eternally grateful to Greene for proving how well Shakespeare was faring as a playwright and, no doubt, as a play doctor. Some believe he 'doctored' *Harey* after Greene and Thomas Nashe had written it.

Chettle, too, pinpoints Shakespeare's growing fame for us, because he made more than an apology, stating how the playwright is praised by 'divers of worship' who have reported his 'uprightness of dealing, which argues his honesty and his facetious [pleasant] grace in writing that approves his art'. After a dearth of facts, this is riches indeed.

The years 1592–4 were plague years in London, 1593 being a time of horror with 11,000 deaths. The theatres were closed for much of the time and Shakespeare turned for some of it to poetry. *Venus and Adonis* was published in 1593 and *The Rape of Lucrece* the following year.

The former, strongly influenced by his beloved Ovid, shot through ten editions in ten years and delighted undergraduates and countless others. It was dedicated to a patron, Henry Wriothesley, 3rd Earl of Southampton (1573–1624), and so was *Lucrece*. The youth was a good friend to writers, and a favourite of the Queen's until he got his friend Essex's cousin, Elizabeth Vernon, with child and married her. This landed him in prison for a short time in 1598, but he went to Ireland with Essex, was recalled, and joined in his friend's disastrous rebellion in 1601, being lucky to escape beheading. He lingered in prison until James I released him.

Southampton loved the theatre and Shakespeare's plays. Apart from the dedications, his links with Shakespeare himself cannot be proved, but few doubt their friendship. Dover Wilson suggests that Shakespeare spent the plague time of 1593–4 at Southampton's home at Titchfield, while tradition – Rowe following Davenant – has the earl giving Shakespeare £1,000.

The sonnets were in full flood during the plague period, the usually accepted dates being 1592–8. But A. L. Rowse, basing his views on his imposingly detailed knowledge of Elizabethan history, dates them 1592–5. These poems, generally assumed to be partly or totally auto-biographical, have spawned a separate Shakespearean industry too vast even to sketch here. They were published in 1609, and the particular mysteries in them are the identities of the dedicatee 'Mr W.H.', the 'lovely boy', the Rival Poet, and the Dark Lady.

Mr W.H. must be either the inspirer of the poems or the procurer of them for publication, for the printer, Thomas Thorpe, wrote of 'the onlie begetter'. Rowse chooses Southampton's stepfather, Sir William Harvey, as procurer (a 'Sir' could be referred to as a Mr), while alleged inspirers include William Herbert, Earl of Pembroke, and Southampton (Henry Wriothesley backwards into W.H.!).

The best bet for the lovely boy must be Southampton, while Marlowe, especially if Rowse's dating is right, is the Rival Poet, though Chapman is more favoured by many scholars. As for the Dark Lady, all was sheerest guesswork until Rowse produced a candidate who would not satisfy a court of law but seems a splendidly likely choice. He produced her with maximum publicity in 1973 in *The Times* and in *Shakespeare the Man*, a dark-complexioned wanton named Emilia Bassano, daughter of a court musician, later married to another musician, Alfonso Lanier. (Actually, Rowse had her married to a William Lanier, but, as he admitted in *The Times* of 2 July 1973, a Miss Mary Edmond put him right about the marriage.)

Emilia was for a time mistress of Shakespeare's Lord Chamberlain and was a poet, too. If she was the Dark Lady, she is a national heroine, not only because of the sonnets, and because of Rosaline in *Love's Labour's Lost*, written at this time, but because finally she was to help inspire Shakespeare's lass unparallel'd, Cleopatra. But at the time of the affair it cannot have comforted him that he could transfigure his feelings later into art. He loved her, lusted after her – wanting his Will in her Hell to use Elizabethan bawdy – and was reduced to the self-disgust of Sonnet 129, which begins: 'The expense of spirit in a waste of shame Is lust in action . . .'

Until Emilia emerged via Dr Rowse from the Bodleian and the papers of the astrologer Simon Forman, the favourite candidate had been Anon, followed closely by Mary Fitton, a Maid of Honour who became Pembroke's mistress. Until someone produces a better candidate than Emilia, Dr Rowse's many 'enemies' might just as well admit that he may be right.

Whatever the pangs of despised love, Shakespeare's professional career was booming, for by 1594 he had finally 'arrived'. With Will Kempe, the Clown, and Richard Burbage, his fellow 'Servantes to the Lord Chamberleyne', he is mentioned in a Council Warrant as being paid for performing at Court.

He was to remain with this supreme company for the rest of his life, though it became the King's Men in 1603 by order of James I. In 1594 he was no longer a hired man, but a sharer, part-owner of the company, taking some of its profit and some of the responsibility for its expenses. At the Globe in 1599 he became a housekeeper as well, which meant he was a part-owner of the actual building. Richard and Cuthbert Burbage owned half of it, while Shakespeare, Augustine Phillips, Thomas Pope, John Heminge and Will Kempe owned half between them. Other companies had a single housekeeper, but not the Globe's band of brothers, who lived so closely together during working hours, and no doubt often out of them, and left each other remembrances of themselves in their wills.

It was his stake in the company, plus extra money from performances at Court, that made Shakespeare rich, that mysterious, perhaps mythical, £1,000 apart. Playwrights made little enough, the meanest payer being Henslowe, who sometimes paid as little as £6 for a play, which became,

The Workes of William Shakespeare

containing all his Comedies, Histories, and
Tragedies : Truely set forth, according to their first
ORIGINALL.

The Names of the Principall Actors
in all these Playes.

William Shakespeare.

Richard Burbadge.

John Hemmings.

Augustine Phillips.

William Kempt.

Thomas Poope.

George Bryan.

Henry Condell.

William Slye.

Richard Cowly.

John Lowine.

Samuell Crosse.

Alexander Cooke.

Samuel Gilburne.

Robert Armin.

William Ostler.

Nathan Field.

John Underwood.

Nicholas Tooley.

William Ecclestone.

Joseph Taylor.

Robert Benfield.

Robert Goughe.

Richard Robinson.

Iohn Shancke.

Iohn Rice.

as was the custom, the joint property of the company. Plays were usually unpublished by their owners, being financially valuable to them, which did not stop pirates scribbling them down and producing corrupt copies. Six of Shakespeare's were pirated. In hard times – the plague years – a company would have some of its plays published, while it is possible that the four of Shakespeare's plays published in 1600 helped to defray the expenses of building the Globe.

Plays were very much working scripts within a company, and it was fortunate that Shakespeare was part of a company, pen at the ready and, as a sharer, responsible for staging plays. These had to be passed by the censor, the Master of the Revels, on the look-out for seditious statements or controversial religious matter.

It is practically impossible to compare incomes today with those in Shakespeare's time, partly because luxuries in one age can be cheap in another: tea is a prime example of this. But if an Elizabethan £1 could be said to equal £25 in the 1970s, and if, as F. E. Halliday suggests, the most Shakespeare ever earned was around £200 a year, that puts him by our reckoning in the £5,000 bracket in some good, plague-free years. During plagues, companies toured and money was tighter. How often Shakespeare went on the road is debatable, for his friends may have let him off to get on with his writing. The last two sonnets suggest he was with them when they played Bath (and took £1), and King Lear's visit to Dover and its cliffs (13s 4d were the company's takings) could be another such example. Touring was tough in plague years or ordinary years, the least unbearable method being on horseback or by waggon on roads or – more usually – non-roads, for most were villainous.

Too much is made of Shakespeare's occasional complaints about the actor's lot. No actor ever lived who did not moan about it from time to time. 'Life's but a walking shadow, a poor player That struts and frets his hour upon the stage And then is heard no more', said Macbeth in pessimistic mood, but only in the sonnets does Shakespeare once or twice bemoan the actor's life so strongly as to make the reader suspect a setback or a very black mood. In No 110 he has made himself 'a motley to the view' and in 111 is almost ashamed of his trade. Even late in the nineteenth century actors were still being snubbed and, as Ivor Brown has suggested, Shakespeare's patron may have been sneered at for consorting with a mere player, and it would be the actor who felt it most.

The Chamberlain's Men were playing at the Theatre in 1594, with the Admiral's Men – and Alleyn – at the Rose. The year 1596 was a proud year for William's father, who got his coat-of-arms, but that August, the worst tragedy of Shakespeare's life occurred, for his only son Hamnet died, aged eleven.

As so often, art was the gainer. Witness Constance's lines in *King John*, almost certainly written soon after:

> Grief fills the room up of my absent child,
> Lies in his bed, walks up and down with me,
> Puts on his pretty looks, repeats his words,
> Remembers me of all his gracious parts,
> Stuffs out his vacant garments with his form;
> Then I have reason to be fond of grief.

And for a man most conscious of his family and line, the blow was a double one.

In October we find him living in Bishopsgate, assessed as owning £5 worth of goods, but by November he had moved south of the river, perhaps to Southwark, for a writ was issued against him by the Sheriff of Surrey after he had fallen out with a JP named Gardiner, later proved to be corrupt.

Despite the death of Hamnet, this was a golden period for Shakespeare, the time of the Histories, including the incomparable *Henry IV*, an unequalled panorama of Tudor England, for all that it is set nearly 200 years earlier. The year 1597 saw him buying New Place in Stratford, the 'Grete House', second largest house in the town. It cost him £60 and, alas, no longer exists.

That September he was acting in Ben Jonson's new play, *Every Man in His Humour*. In the Folio* of his friend's plays (1616) he heads the list of 'principal comedians', and Rowe has it that it was Shakespeare who got his company to stage the play in the first place.

In 1598, Frances Meres, scholar of both Oxford and Cambridge, put future generations in his debt by publishing his *Palladis Tamia: Wit's Treasury*, a look at English literature since Chaucer. Not only did he

---

* Folio and Quarto are both printing terms. Here they refer respectively to a collection of plays in one volume and a (handy) edition of a single play.

characterise Shakespeare as 'honey-tongued' and place him as 'most excellent' in comedy and tragedy and among the best lyric poets, but he listed a number of plays, thus proving that they had already been produced. His evidence will be cited in Chapter 4, but one play will not be there, *Love's Labour's Won*. This was thought to have been another name for *The Taming of the Shrew*, but a recently found contemporary list in which both are mentioned has disproved this. It is either a lost play or, perhaps, another name for *All's Well*. *Much Ado* and *Troilus and Cressida* have also been put forward, the last by Leslie Hotson, who believes that the title really means 'love's pains earned'. Perhaps somewhere in some library or attic lies the answer . . .

In 1598, *Love's Labour's Lost* was published, with Shakespeare's name attached to a play for the first time, while in the same year the Stratford Town Council paid the poet 10p for a load of stone. From such minutiae is Shakespearean biography assembled.

The next year the most famous of all theatres, the Globe, was built in suitably dramatic circumstances. The lease was up for the Theatre, and Cuthbert Burbage, having failed to negotiate a new one with the owner, Giles Allen, decided to pull it down and transport the wood across the river to the South Bank.

The outraged Allen, in a later court case, described how the Burbages and 'divers others' armed themselves with all sorts of 'unlawful and offensive weapons', proceeded to the playhouse, pulled it down and carried all the 'wood and timber thereof' to Bankside. Not only did Allen fail to get the £800 he wanted, but he was also refused 40 shillings compensation for his trampled-upon grass. Meanwhile, Burbage and company had the joy of seeing their new theatre rising near Maiden Lane. It was the most easterly of the four playhouses on Bankside.

Before the Globe was completed, Essex and Southampton had gone to Ireland to fight the rebels there, an event mentioned by the Chorus at the start of Act V of *Henry V*, a rare case of a Shakespeare play being easy to date. And that Autumn Thomas Platter of Basle saw *Julius Caesar* at the new playhouse. His account of it included a mention of 'the jig that followed the play'. This was standard practice and not to Shakespeare's liking. Jigs were skits, often topical, which included songs and dances. They died with the closing of the theatres in the 1640s, but the idea of following even a major tragedy with something lighter was resurrected. (As late as Irving's time, the most lightweight farce often followed a supreme masterpiece.)

In 1600, the Admiral's Men moved to the new Fortune, hoping to challenge the Globe's success. The Fortune Theatre was in Finsbury; it was burnt down in 1621, rebuilt with brick, then finally dismantled in 1649.

Essex's foolhardy rebellion in February 1601 involved Shakespeare and his friends, for supporters of the impetuous earl asked the Chamberlain's Men to revive *Richard II*, hoping to gain support for the deposing of one monarch by showing another's downfall on the stage. The day chosen was the very day before the uprising. Later, Augustine Phillips had the alarming job of explaining the players' involvement to the authorities, but they were not blamed and, in fact, found themselves acting before the Queen the day before Essex was beheaded. With Southampton in prison, it is reasonable to suppose that if Shakespeare was in the cast his mind was not entirely on his work.

His father was buried on 8 September, having lived to see his fortunes restored thanks to his brilliant son. This may have been the year of *Twelfth Night* and *Troilus and Cressida*, that bitter, cynical, fascinating and amusing play so concerned with the need for duty, order and authority. Achilles has been seen as Essex, who has also been cast less logically as Hamlet. It must have been an unsettling year for Shakespeare, emotionally tied to the Essex faction but profoundly believing in the *status quo*.

In 1602, he bought 127 acres of land in Old Stratford for £320, his brother Gilbert the haberdasher arranging the big transaction. Later in the year he bought the copyhold of a cottage opposite New Place.

Meanwhile, back in London, a splendid story was being told about him, a good sign of success, whether it is true or not. According to John Manningham of the Middle Temple, a woman, after seeing Burbage play Richard III, made an assignation with him for that night. It was arranged that he should announce himself at her door in the name of his part. Shakespeare overheard this, got there first, and was 'intertained, and at his game ere Burbage came'. Word being brought that Richard III was at the door, Shakespeare sent down a message – 'William the Conqueror was before Richard III'.

On 24 March 1603 Gloriana died, leaving a stupendous void in nature for a while, even though she had begun to outlive her age. Shakespeare and other poets were called on by a ballad-maker to lament her in verse, but he did not – was it because of Southampton and Essex? – leaving it until his last play, *Henry VIII*, to do her justice. There was no need, with a Stuart on the throne, to put such a paean of prophetic praise into Cranmer's mouth as he christened the royal infant, but by 1613 the greatest figure of the age (though no one yet knew it) could salute the second greatest as she so richly deserved.

James VI of Scotland, now James I of England, was the answer to an actor's prayer. His passion for the theatre had been frustrated in a land where it was outlawed. No doubt encouraged by his theatre-loving wife, Anne of Denmark, he forced the Kirk Sessions to allow Fletcher's players to perform in Edinburgh in 1599. Some believe that Shakespeare and his colleagues visited Scotland after the *Richard II* incident, where he picked up information for *Macbeth*. There is no proof.

Whether he had seen the Chamberlain's Men before or not, James at once translated them into the King's Men. They became Grooms of the Chamber, entitled to wear royal livery.

That winter Shakespeare acted in Jonson's *Sejanus*, the last record we have of his acting. He is listed in the 1616 Folio text second to Burbage. And, also that winter, plague closed the theatres.

The King went to Wilton House in Wiltshire, the home of the Earl of Pembroke, and the King's Men were summoned to entertain him. In 1865, William Cory, the poet, was told by Lady Herbert that there was a letter from Lady Pembroke to her son at Wilton House, which had never been printed. It contained two pieces of information. It is interesting that the play performed was *As You Like It*; it is sheer electricity that the Countess wrote in the missing letter: 'We have the man Shakespeare with us.' That is how aristocratic theatre fans down the centuries have regarded successful, interesting show people – with a mixture of patronage and admiring fascination.

Shakespeare took part in James's Coronation Procession, neatly kitted out in newly supplied red cloth. He was now living in Silver Street, Cripplegate, lodging with Christopher Mountjoy and his wife, who were Huguenots. Mountjoy made tires (ornamental headpieces) for ladies, including the Queen.

Liked by his friends and acquaintances, financially secure, and at the very height of his powers – for it was the time of the great tragedies – this was Shakespeare's high summer.

His elder daughter Susanna married Dr John Hall in 1607. It was a good match. From her epitaph, noted in 1707 before the stone's inscription was erased, she seems to have been as delightful as her father, and Hall, allowing for the dismal medical standards of his day, was a highly regarded master of his alarming craft. A daughter was born to the Halls in 1608, the only grandchild Shakespeare lived to enjoy. His mother died that year and, professionally, a major event took place. The King's Men took over the leading private (indoors) theatre, the Blackfriars. This was the first time that adults, as opposed to 'little eyases', had performed regularly in a private theatre. Receipts were higher because of higher prices, and there was no interference from the weather. Shakespeare was a housekeeper with a seventh of the shares.

Productions were more elaborate in the private theatres, with more scenery, and more comfortable seats; candle-lit evening performances were the fashion. Shakespeare's later plays were geared to the indoors theatre and were influenced by the Court masques which were growing in popularity, extravaganzas of acting, singing and dancing, performed by amateurs, but staged and designed by professionals, the most notable being Ben Jonson and Inigo Jones. Shakespeare's masques, in early and late plays, were, of course, professional to the hilt. Ironically, though the King's Men and the other companies were still forced by public opinion to use boys in female parts, ladies of the Court could take part in Court masques.

The stages of the private theatres are as much of a mystery as the public stages. There was no proscenium arch, at least in Shakespeare's day, but a real difference was the seating, with rows of benches where groundlings would normally have stood. How far the stage thrust out is unknown.

Around 1610 Shakespeare retired to live in Stratford, but he remained one of the King's Men and continued to write for them. In 1613, he bought 'the Gatehouse' in Blackfriars for £140, mortgaging it the next day for £60. It was his only London investment. Presumably he was present at the Globe when it was burnt down on 29 June during the première of *Henry VIII*. It cost him and the other housekeepers £1,400 to rebuild.

An entry in the Stratford Corporation accounts at Christmas 1614 records payment of 20 pence for a quart of sack and a quart of 'clarrett wine' for the entertainment of a preacher at New Place. Dramatic entertainments were not favoured in Stratford at this time, the puritanical authorities having banned players in 1602 and not revoked the ban. The irony of Shakespeare's position in the town is beyond comment.

The last years of his life were eventful on the domestic front. First Susanna ran into trouble, then, three years later, in 1616, it was Judith's turn.

Susanna's was less long-term. She was forced to sue one John Lane who had alleged that she '. . . had the runninge of the raynes [wore the trousers at home] and had been "naught" with Rafe Smith'. Lane failed to appear in court and was excommunicated. 'Witty above her sexe' ran Susanna's epitaph, which noted that she wept with others and cheered them up. She seems an unlikely candidate for adultery with Rafe Smith: she was 'wise to salvation' – good.

We know more about Judith's problems. She was unmarried at thirty-one, on the shelf with a vengeance by Elizabethan and Jacobean standards. However, she found a man, Thomas Quiney, a vintner four years younger than herself, and the son of a friend of her father's. They married, but got themselves excommunicated for doing so out of season, at a time of year when a licence should have been obtained.

Two months later all was explained when Quiney was had up for carnal intercourse with a Margaret Wheeler, who had now died in childbirth. Had Quiney rapidly got married to Judith to avoid doing his duty by Margaret, thinking Shakespeare's daughter the better catch? He had not reckoned with his father-in-law. Shakespeare would hardly adopt too moral an attitude in view of his own past, but he must have thought Quiney a poor specimen, so altered his will, thereby depriving Judith of money which would have gone straight to Quiney by law. True, she got a marriage portion, but if she died within three years the money would go to his grandchild and his sister, Joan Hart.

He signed his final will on 25 March and a very conventional document it was, whatever sensation-mongers have said of it. Items included 26s 8d each for his 'ffelowes John Hemynge Richard Burbage & Henry Cundell' to buy rings in remembrance of him, and £10 for the Stratford poor. It was Heminge and Condell who were to ensure his immortality by publishing the First Folio in 1623, which included no less than eighteen unpublished plays. The chief beneficiary was Susanna, though Anne automatically got standard widow's rights, and Joan the house in Henley Street, plus all her brother's 'wearing Apparell'.

He died on 23 April 1616 and was buried on the 25th. Only one tradition survives about his death, written down by Parson Ward, vicar of Stratford from 1662 to 1681. Strangely, it is not an unhappy one, for all its sad ending, because it rings so true of the theatre and of what we know of Shakespeare's reputation for good fellowship. He had been drinking with his old friends Ben Jonson and Michael Drayton, the Warwickshire poet who was later to be cured of a fever by Shakespeare's son-in-law. Dr Hall could not cure the fever that Shakespeare is said to have caught after that no doubt splendid last party.

So he was 'i' th' way to study a long silence', as his great contemporary, John Webster, put it in *The White Devil*. Brightness had fallen from the air and the world was left with dazzling masterpieces that are one of mankind's supreme achievements, a few facts about their creator, and a number of portraits, most of them suspect.

Brushing aside the monument in Holy Trinity Church which, though it must contain something of the look of the man, is less believable than the average bad passport photograph, we are left with only one portrait that is generally accepted as negatively reliable. This is the engraving by Droeshout in the First Folio. Sentimentalists who secretly and absurdly half hope that all poets look like Byron, who innocently believe that the face is the man, rail against the engraving. They should ask any actor what some strong silent men of integrity are like off stage and screen, and learn how some gross character man has the heart of a poet.

Not that the Droeshout is more than a rough approximation of what Shakespeare looked like. It was not done from life, but probably from a copy of one that was, and it is a poor work of art. But Jonson gave it his blessing, and anyone with imagination can gaze at it and deduce a man of sensibility and rare intelligence. The other portraits have their defenders and every Shakespearean has his favourite; but let Ben Jonson have the last word – 'reader, look Not on his picture, but his book'.

Photographic copy of the proof impression of DROESHOUT'S PORTRAIT of SHAKESPEARE, 1623, from the unique original in the possession of J.O. HALLIWELL esq.

Page 51 (*above*) The Droeshout portrait of Shakespeare; (*below*) Hall's Croft, the home of Shakespeare's daughter Susanna and her husband, Dr John Hall

Page 52 (*above*) Anne Hathaway's Cottage at Shottery; (*below*) Mary Arden's house at Wilmcote

3

THE ARTIST-CRAFTSMAN

The applause! delight! the wonder of our Stage! – Ben Jonson

Shakespeare lives! But why? It is standard practice to glory in the poetry and drama of the Elizabethans and Jacobeans, but precious little of it gets read after schooldays are over, or performed professionally. Many of the plays which were once so popular have become Interesting Historical Monuments, with no sign that they will experience the revival that has happened to Monteverdi – or early Verdi.

True, over a decade a Londoner at least can collect rarities like *'Tis Pity She's a Whore*, *The Changeling* and *A Chaste Maid in Cheapside*; and *The Revenger's Tragedy* can be splendidly dropped into the Stratford and Aldwych repertoires with a guaranteed audience. Jacobean attitudes strike a chord with listeners today, but Ford, Middleton and Tourneur and the rest are more honoured in the textbook than on the stage.

Even Marlowe, for all his genius, does not often fully live for us. He did when Tyrone Guthrie directed *Tamburlaine* at the Old Vic in 1951, with Donald Wolfit, a Mongol horde in himself, as the superhuman hero. 'Kit, my boy, we've done it!' exulted Wolfit off-stage after the first night, and they had. But such a play needs supermen to perform it: most Shakespeare can survive in schools and village halls. *Edward II* lives if its hero is remarkable, *Faustus* – just – by its verse, and *The Jew of Malta* if treated as a horror comic *con brio*.

Ben Jonson has strong academic support and several great comedies to his credit. His genius for caricature is often compared to Dickens's, but Westminster, his birthplace, could hardly be made into a Stratford unless *Volpone*, *The Alchemist* and *Bartholomew Fair*, etc were fabulously cast. His greatness and historical importance are unquestioned, but that is not our concern here.

Only one playwright of the age of glory truly crosses the centuries, as Shakespeare does. He is John Webster, about whom almost nothing is known, but whose *The Duchess of Malfi* and *The White Devil* still hypnotise audiences, fascinated by their evil but magnificent worlds, and made breathless by the power of their author's language. Indeed, *The Duchess of Malfi* is probably the most popular non-Shakespearean play of its era. Webster's sombre, tragic, diseased vision inspired pessimistic lines to match Shakespeare's, and Ferdinand's 'Cover her face; mine eyes dazzle: she died young', as he looks down on his dead sister, the Duchess, has never been excelled by anyone.

But Webster's output was small, and, with a brief salute to Dekker's *The Shoemaker's Holiday*, which can be vastly entertaining if done well, and Massinger's *A New Way to Pay Old Debts*, in which Edmund Kean sent Lord Byron into a convulsion, we are back where we began, with Shakespeare.

He does not live by his perfection. No one could attain that at all times, at the speed he worked. He did occasionally revise, whatever Heminge and Condell might write about never blotting a line, but being seemingly unbothered by visions of immortality he was not much concerned with polishing of plays, even when he may have had the time. A careless moment, noted by Nevill Coghill in his *Shakespeare's Professional Skills*, will serve as illustration. Says Viola in *Twelfth Night* to the Captain before she goes to Orsino:

> Thou shalt present me as an Eunuch to him,
> It may be worth thy pains: for I can sing . . .

And who sings in the play? Feste alone. There are two explanations, one that a boy's voice broke, the other that Robert Armin, the Feste, could sing well. Whichever is right, it was careless not to remove Viola's remark.

Some critics, incidentally, see other hands helping Shakespeare where the verse is less than extraordinary, an astonishing indication of their failure to understand the pressures under which he worked.

His greatness as a poet would not in itself have made him live, especially into our unpoetically-inclined age, and would not account for his hold on millions who know no English. And it is not enough to say he was sublime. It may be true, but it takes us back to Victorian times when heroes like Beethoven and Shakespeare were hailed for their moral grandeur (the latter's bawdy having been misunderstood or safely bowdlerised). So why does he live?

First, because of his genius in telling a story. He was a born story-teller. Nevill Coghill, probably surprising those who even now cannot relate Shakespeare to the stage, claims it was his 'primal starting-point . . . he ransacked history and fiction for stories that could be made significant and told, or re-told, upon a stage. He was a supreme stage storyteller and perceived that the basic source of all meaning that can be presented though his medium was the image of a human action'. Let those wise words comfort Shakespeareans when they are faced with directors who try to 'improve' the plays because they do not trust their stories. Let them comfort readers who have to endure lesser dramatic critics trying to make a name for boldness by damning an astonishing number of them as silly.

Shakespeare's narrative skill is all the more effective because so many of his stories are universal in their appeal, and he was born with a genius for scene-building, a genius now much more fully recognised because, as has been mentioned, modern staging is at last recapturing the speed of Elizabethan performances by cutting out slow scene changes of realistic scenery.

Linked with the story in many of the plays is a theme, revenge in *Hamlet*, pride in *Coriolanus*, honour in *Henry IV*, jealousy in *Othello*, and springing from the stories is the most wonderful array of characters in fiction, a teeming world in which the tiniest may have his moment. It is hardly fair to such moments of mastery to note them out of context, but many can stand on their own . . .

At the climax of the revels towards the end of *Love's Labour's Lost*, a messenger named Mercade breaks in to speak to the Princess of France:

> *Mercade*: God save you, madam!
> *Princess*: Welcome, Mercade;
> But that thou interrupt'st our merriment.
> *Mercade*: I am sorry, madam; for the news I bring
> Is heavy in my tongue. The king your father –
> *Princess*: Dead, for my life!
> *Mercade*: Even so: my tale is told.
> *Berowne*: Worthies, away! The scene begins to cloud.

After Berowne's haunting line Mercade exits, having completed the best minute part in Shakespeare.

In the great Tavern scene in *Henry IV Part 1* – Act II Scene IV – there is a character called Francis, who is a drawer (a tapster). He has a few words as he bustles in and out, most of them being 'Anon, anon, sir' and he is unforgettable.

In *Antony and Cleopatra*, unnamed soldiers on guard hear music as the play is heading for its tragic climax:

> *Fourth Soldier*: Peace! what noise?
> *First Soldier*: List, list!
> *Second Soldier*: Hark!
> *First Soldier*: Music i' the air.
> *Third Soldier*: Under the earth.
> *Fourth Soldier*: It signs well, does it not?
> *Third Soldier*: No.
> *First Soldier*: Peace, I say! What should this mean?
> *Second Soldier*: 'Tis the god Hercules, whom Antony lov'd,
> Now leaves him.

And in the same play, at the very beginning, Philo, a friend of Antony's who has only three more lines and does not appear in any other scene, opens the play with this incomparable piece of scene-setting. To Demetrius he says bitterly:

> Nay, but this dotage of our general's
> O'erflows the measure; those his goodly eyes,
> That o'er the files and musters of the war
> Have glow'd like plated Mars, now bend, now turn
> The office and devotion of their view
> Upon a tawny front: his captain's heart,
> Which in the scuffles of great fights hath burst
> The buckles on his breast, reneges all temper,
> And is become the bellows and the fan
> To cool a gipsy's lust. Look! where they come.
>
> (*Antony and Cleopatra enter with their attendants*)
>
> Take but good note, and you shall see in him
> The triple pillar of the world transform'd
> Into a strumpet's fool; behold and see.

If the beginning of *Hamlet* is, as some have claimed, the most exciting opening in drama, surely Philo's speech is the most remarkable.

One more moment will suffice out of a score more to show how Shakespeare's mastery extended to the smallest fry. In *The Winter's Tale* the Third Gentleman reports to his friends on the reunion of the two kings and of Leontes and his daughter Perdita. His description, all affected speech at first, of how Perdita was suddenly overcome with emotion, includes this:

> . . . she did, with an 'alas!' I would fain say, bleed tears, for I am sure my heart wept blood.

For many theatregoers and readers, Shakespeare's characters, major and minor, are the main attraction of the plays, though, like his poetry, prose and imagery, they all spring from his stories and themes and are part of them. Hamlet and Macbeth, Falstaff and Hotspur, Beatrice and Benedick and scores of others are so vividly drawn that many, without affectation, regard them as real people. Though, as we shall see, there are scholars who oppose this harmless, eminently sane view, it should be admitted that even Shakespeare did not create every type of person, though his range exceeds any other dramatist of his own or any day. There is no saint to be found in his plays, partly because of the censorship problem, partly, perhaps, by inclination. And there is no popular outlaw figure, sympathetically drawn, a Robin Hood – or a Che Guevara. Jack Cade is fascinating, but no hero in *Henry VI*.

The gap is hardly surprising, for he was no lover of mobs and their leaders (*Julius Caesar, Coriolanus*). Yet his sympathy with the individual commoner, indeed the individual of all classes, is apparent everywhere. Perhaps the gentleman of Stratford seems sometimes a little patronising to modern tastes, but who could deny the respect of the playwright for his creation Corin in *As You Like It*:

> Sir, I am a true labourer: I earn that I eat, get that I wear, owe no man hate, envy no man's happiness, glad of other men's good, content with my harm; and the greatest of my pride is to see my ewes graze and my lambs suck.

Shakespeare laughs with, not at, bully Bottom and his friends. Only in the equivalent scene in *Love's Labour's Lost* is there a slightly sour edge to the humour. In the *Dream*, Theseus takes all the sting out of the teasing by saying: 'For never anything can be amiss When simpleness and duty tender it.' And the knowingness of the ordinary man – First Gravedigger, Autolycus and a host of others – is given full rein. So is his suffering when a soldier: witness Williams and his argument the night before Agincourt with the disguised King Henry.

Despite the difficulty inherent in relying on boy actors, the gallery of women in Shakespeare's plays is staggering in its variety, from Cleopatra, through the practical, good-natured, tender and forgiving heroines, to Mrs Quickly and the splendid Mistress Overdone, who has had nine husbands, but been overdone by the last, as Pompey reports.

Shakespeare the poetic dramatist developed fast. In the early plays verse was often merely decorative, if delightful, as with Benvolio's

> Madam, an hour before the worshipp'd sun
> Peer'd forth the golden window of the east.

Yet in the play (*Romeo and Juliet*) the greatest creation is Mercutio, a prose man in the main, like many of Shakespeare's early character successes.

Almost from the start, though, Shakespeare learnt to use verse for true characterisation as well as beauty (Richard III, Berowne, etc), and in *Romeo* he anticipated later mastery. Capulet has some fine functional verse at his ball in the speech beginning:

> Welcome, gentlemen! ladies that have their toes
> Unplagu'd with corns will walk a bout with you.
> Ah ha! my mistresses, which of you all
> Will now deny to dance? she that makes dainty, she,
> I'll swear, hath corns; am I come near ye now?

From *Henry IV* to *Twelfth Night* verse often takes second place to prose, yet Shakespeare was swiftly learning how to handle, and channel his genius for, dramatic poetry. Though in the first *Henry IV* play we have the King intoning so heavily at times that only a very good actor can make him live, Hotspur reveals the poet's growing mastery of dramatic verse from his opening scene, 'My liege, I did deny no prisoners . . .' A later speech proclaims the new, amazing flexibility:

> Why, look you, I am whipp'd and scourg'd with rods,
> Nettled, and stung with pismires, when I hear
> Of this vile politician, Bolingbroke.
> In Richard's time – what do ye call the place? –
> A plague upon't – it is in Gloucestershire; –
> 'Twas where the madcap duke his uncle kept,
> His uncle York; where first I bow'd my knee
> Unto this king of smiles, this Bolingbroke,
> 'Sblood!
> When you and he came back from Ravenspurgh.

After the variety of speeches like that – and Hotspur has plenty of them – anything was possible. The later plays embraced every style to perfection. 'Where the bee sucks' and other lovely, simple lyrics were not banished if the time was right, and there was still plenty of apt prose, but the verse was now ranging from effective to incomparable. The supreme scenes reached unexcelled heights. Such a scene is Act III Scene III of *Othello*, culminating in the Moor howling for blood, a vengeance duet, a short speech of Othello's beginning with the verbal agony of 'Damn her, lewd minx! O, damn her!', then Iago's ultimate, ironic, brazen statement: 'I am your own for ever.'

In the great tragedies the purplest passages never rely on beauty for its own sake, even the ultimate aria, Enobarbus's description of Cleopatra, because the description is vital to our understanding of the plot. Besides, the Master breaks the spell in masterly fashion. Agrippa comments earthily:

> Royal wench!
> She made great Caesar lay his sword to bed;
> He plough'd her, and she cropp'd.

The simple, unexplainable truth is that Shakespeare's command of language became total – and unique.

Part of this mastery, though last in dramatic importance, was his matchless imagery. Conventional enough in the early plays and poems, it grew with observation and finally could take in a whole vivid pattern of verbal pictures, not simply isolated flashes. As Professor Halliday has pointed out, in a most famous speech of Prospero, 'the dissolution of the great *globe* is related to our little life *rounded* with a sleep'.

> The solemn temples, the great globe itself,
> Yea, all which it inherit, shall dissolve
> And, like this insubstantial pageant faded,
> Leave not a wrack behind. We are such stuff
> As dreams are made on, and our little life
> Is rounded with a sleep.

An early student of Shakespeare's imagery was Walter Whiter in his *Specimen of a Commentary on Shakespeare* (1794). He showed that Shakespeare's mind always linked certain ideas: flatterers made him think of dogs, while dogs conjured up sweetmeats. Hotspur says of Bolingbroke (just after the speech quoted earlier):

> Why, what a candy deal of courtesy
> This fawning greyhound then did proffer me!

while in *Antony and Cleopatra*, Antony laments:

> All come to this? The hearts
> That spaniel'd me at heels, to whom I gave
> Their wishes, do discandy, melt their sweets
> On blossoming Caesar.

A whole industry later grew up around the imagery, partly as a reaction to A. C. Bradley's classic *Shakespearean Tragedy* (1904) in which the characters were treated as real people, not merely dramatic creations. A major attack was launched on Bradley by L. C. Knights in 1933 in *How Many Children Had Lady Macbeth?*, a question Bradley had asked in an appendix. Knights wanted the plays considered strictly as dramatic poems. But the most famous study of Shakespeare's imagery appeared in 1935 in Caroline Spurgeon's book of that title. She found that while some symbolic imagery occurred in all the plays, some of them had their own particular imagery. *Hamlet* reveals imagery about disease and sickness, *Romeo and Juliet* has an extraordinary number of images about light. *Hamlet*, indeed, introduces sickness in the first few lines – ' 'tis bitter cold And I am sick at heart' – and the Ghost has some memorable phrases, 'leperous distilment' and 'lazar-like' being two related ones. A memorable cluster of light images in *Romeo* has him telling Juliet:

> Night's candles are burnt out, and jocund day
> Stands tiptoe on the misty mountain tops.

Unfortunately, Miss Spurgeon found too much of Shakespeare the Man in the imagery. No one could deny that he was less than a perfect dog-lover, but to state (as she did) that he blushed easily and disliked noise is to fall into the trap of forgetting – one must never forget it – Shakespeare's unique skill in creating different people. The truth, as Professor Halliday has so aptly put it, is that character and poetry are equally important for they are the same thing.

The popularity of the plays down the years is dealt with in the next chapter, while dates and sources are discussed in Appendix 1. To finish this chapter there follows a very brief guide to the plays.

The Comedy of Errors, if it is, as many experts now believe, the earliest of the plays, is an amazingly skilful piece, short, farcical and enjoyable. Getting his plot from Plautus, Shakespeare gave his play unity of time and nearly of place. Two pairs of identical twins are a good start for any mechanical farce, though there is emotion in the play, even grief at the start. That Shakespeare could not yet handle romantic love convincingly is perhaps proved by a long rhyming speech of Antipholus of Syracuse. Part of it runs:

> Sing, siren, for thyself and I will dote:
> Spread o'er the silver waves thy golden hair
> And as a bed I'll take them and there lie,
> And in that glorious supposition think
> He gains by death that hath such means to die.

But the play works in the theatre and that is what matters.

So does *Titus Andronicus*, as we have known since Peter Brook's famous 1955 production at Stratford. This tragedy, inspired by Seneca, can no longer be written off as a chapter of horrors and carnage. Not that some of the horrors are not enjoyable, partly because Aaron is such a splendid villain. One's heart warms to a man who, buried 'breast-deep in earth' and then starved to death, laments only that he cannot perform other deeds, 'ten thousand worse than ever yet I did'.

Titus is a true tragic hero, though his endless misfortunes make heavy demands on an actor's skill in obtaining endless variety. Signs of future power and glory include Titus's

> If there were reason for these miseries,
> Then into limits could I bind my woes.
> When heaven doth weep, doth not the earth o'erflow?
> If the winds rage, doth not the sea wax mad,
> Threat'ning the welkin with his big-swoln face?
> And wilt thou have a reason for this coil?
> I am the sea; hark! how her signs do blow;
> She is the weeping welkin, I the earth:
> Then must my sea be moved with her sighs;
> Then must my earth with her continual tears
> Become a deluge, overflow'd and drown'd.

There may have followed the three parts of *Henry VI*, then, as a culmination, the first masterpiece, *Richard III*. The playwright's development is swift. Part 1 of *Henry VI* is naïve and rhetorical, but workmanlike, with Shakespeare well able to use sources, able to create a hero, Talbot, able to use rhymed couplets effectively, as in Talbot's speech over his dead son:

> Come, come, and lay him in his father's arms:
> My spirit can no longer bear these harms.
> Soldiers, adieu! I have what I would have,
> Now my old arms are young John Talbot's grave.

Some affirm that Shakespeare wrote the whole play, others that he completed it. Neither case can be proved. Every page of Part 2 shows some sign of growing mastery and powers of characterisation: poor King Henry, Queen Margaret, Jack Cade's men, and York, who in Part 3 characterises the Queen as 'O tiger's heart wrapt in a woman's hide!' In the third play Shakespeare shows an England torn by civil war, a Tudor looking back on an old nightmare. And he creates a wonderfully simple symbolic scene. At Towton, Henry soliloquises on the 'fell war', then watches and listens to a son who has killed his father and a father who has killed his son. And ever-growing is the menace of Gloucester, who is soon to blossom into the sardonic Satan rampant of *Richard III*. 'There is no creature loves me' he laments before his last battle, but millions of playgoers would dispute it.

Though by later standards too many of the parts are shadowy, it is less of a one-part play than some claim. Clarence and Buckingham are splendid roles, and Lady Anne shares one of the most electrifying scenes in drama with Richard, as he turns her seething hatred into hypnotised love, then, having won her and seen her go, memorably and blandly states: 'I'll have her, but I will not keep her long.' Funny, frightening, proud and sinfully clever, he is Shakespeare's first masterpiece.

The Taming of the Shrew is both vigorous and effective. Even before 'women's lib', Petruchio's swaggering and brazen methods hardly qualified him as an ideal hero, but he is a man of common sense and uncommon gusto, and Shakespeare plays fair with his Shrew. Her violence is mainly due to jealousy of her sister Bianca, whom she knows her father prefers and other men find more attractive. For all the horseplay, the relationship between Petruchio and Katharina is a true one.

The Two Gentlemen of Verona is a romantic comedy, with Shakespeare presumably learning how young aristocrats behaved from swift observation and/or from his reading of John Lyly. The play's theme of friendship being finer than love could not spark off a major success at this moment in his career, and it ranks as one of the least known and – by Shakespearean standards – least interesting. Yet the faithful Julia has some fine verse, 'Who is Silvia?' is a beautiful song, there are moments of fine inspiration, and there is Crab, the splendidly sour-natured dog of Launce. His master's opening speech about him deserves quoting in full or not at all, and space forbids it in full. Later he asks his cur: 'When didst thou see me heave up my leg and make water against a gentlewoman's farthingale? Didst thou ever see me do such a trick?' Crab refuses to answer. Shakespeare was already a master of low comedy.

The closure of the theatres from the plague may have helped make him a master of poetry, for *Venus and Adonis*, *The Rape of Lucrece* and, in particular, the Sonnets, so increased his poetic powers that of the next four plays, two were masterpieces, one is considered by many to be one, and the fourth is at least intensely interesting.

The possible masterpiece is *Love's Labour's Lost* and even its less ardent admirers will allow that it was an amazing achievement for a young playwright. It is a comedy of manners with plenty of action and wit. If the vow of the four young men to forswear women for a fixed period and concentrate on study is improbable, though based on some sort of fact, it triggers off verbal splendour and much fun. With Berowne (Biron), Shakespeare gives us his first Shakespeare Man, that short line of glory referred to in the previous chapter (pages 23–4).

Berowne is a first sketch for another Shakespeare Man, Benedick, while his Rosaline anticipates Beatrice, certainly a supreme Shakespeare Woman. The play is full of good parts, but the number of topical jokes and some complicated (to modern ears) language require clever playing. The pedantic schoolmaster Holofernes in particular is by no means actor-proof. Yet the play enchants if properly done.

King John is flawed but fascinating. It is diffuse, too many themes affecting its hold on an audience. But the Bastard Faulconbridge is a major – and very entertaining – creation whether involved in the action or making chorus-like comments on it. At the very end he has a patriotic purple passage, but finer is a moment in battle. He enters with Austria's head, Austria whom he has been taunting earlier. Wearily he says:

> Now, by my life, this day grows wondrous hot;
> Some airy devil hovers in the sky
> And pours down mischief. Austria's head lie there
> While Philip breathes.

Constance's fine lament over her son was noted in Chapter 2 in connection with Shakespeare's loss of his own son. Shakespeare mocks her madness a little, but not there. John, guilty and treacherous, is finely drawn. 'Within me is a hell' he laments at his death, and earlier he has had a classic exchange with Hubert over the intended fate of the boy Arthur:

> *John*: Death.
> *Hubert*: My Lord?
> *John*: A grave.
> *Hubert*: He shall not live.

Many good playwrights do not achieve anything as fine as that exchange in a lifetime.

With *Richard II*, total mastery is achieved and a new figure is introduced to English tragedy, for Richard is brought down by flaws in his own character. He grows as a man as his fortunes crumble away after he has allowed his sensitive, intelligent nature to become warped by self-indulgence and self-dramatisation, even claiming that his situation is worse than Christ's after Judas had betrayed him. And he is incompetent, weak and egotistical until the end when courage and nobility come to him. His patriotism is never in doubt: like others in the play, he is obsessed by the very earth of England. His speeches are famed for lyrical beauty, even though old John of Gaunt gets the play's most famous one, 'This royal throne of kings . . .'

Bolingbroke is the efficient man of action who topples him, but he will suffer for the crime of taking a throne in *Henry IV*. The play is short on humour and is not so stocked with vivid characters as the later Histories, but it is a major work of art.

So is *Romeo and Juliet*. The fate of its lovers is written in the stars, though Romeo's wild impetuosity, the result of his passion, helps intensify a tragedy triggered off by events. Such passionate intensity must be disastrous, Shakespeare shows us, especially in the volcanic atmosphere of a feud-ridden Verona. Now he was a supreme *dramatic* poet. The extreme lyricism of the verse is sometimes merely decorative but, like great *bel canto* arias, it nearly always adds to the emotion. In the middle of an aria urgently pleading the same theme, Juliet urges:

> Come, night! come, Romeo: come thou day in night,
>
> . . . .
>
> Come, gentle night; come, loving, black-brow'd night
> Give me my Romeo.

The later Shakespeare might have added more solid matter to such a speech, might have intensified even Romeo's last speech, but we should be grateful he wrote the play when he did when lyric splendour reaches the heights of:

> O my love! my wife!
> Death, that hath suck'd the honey of thy breath,
> Hath had no power yet upon thy beauty:

> Thou art not conquer'd; beauty's ensign yet
> Is crimson in thy lips and in thy cheeks,
> And death's pale flag is not advanced there.

It is a commonplace to say that Mercutio is the best male part in the play. He overshadows Romeo while he lives, because in him Shakespeare combined Renaissance Man with Shakespeare Man to supreme effect. Besides, Romeo is a very difficult part which rarely makes an actor's name. He has one moment which is sheer impossibility. In Mantua he hears of Juliet's death, sums up his feelings in a single line, then gets down to business. It is a rare case of Shakespeare being unfair to an actor:

> Is it even so? then I defy you, stars!
> Thou knowst my lodging: get me ink and paper
> And hire post-horses; I will hence tonight.

Shakespeare gives him a final speech which is a magnificent affirmation of life without any self-pity; the excerpt quoted from it above, beginning 'O my love!', does not show Romeo sorry for himself. The dramatist gives Juliet simply a great part, not least because of the growing sense of isolation in which she finds herself. Her position is pitiful and truly tragic.

Proof of Shakespeare's new maturity is the wealth of good parts in the play, not simply the famous roles like Mercutio and the Nurse, but 'spitfire' Tybalt, the 'prince of cats'; young Benvolio; that stern but loving Tudor father, old Capulet; the Prince of Verona; and, given a very good actor, even Friar Laurence who, at the play's end, states he will be brief and is anything but.

A Midsummer Night's Dream, its plot apparently invented by Shakespeare, is an adored romantic comedy. Shakespeare creates several worlds in one, and several languages: the formal speech of Theseus and his bride-to-be; the lovers, who often slide into rhyming couplets; the varying speech of the fairy world; and the splendid prose of Bottom and his friends except when they burst into bad verse in *Pyramus and Thisbe*. All these different worlds are peopled by a wealth of characters who are loved by playgoers, but it must be said that the Polish scholar, Jan Kott, in his very influential *Shakespeare Our Contemporary*, finds an ugly world, full of slimy creatures, spotted snakes, spiders and devils, far away from the Warwickshire countryside and Mendelssohn's music. Though this misreading of the enchanted forest – Mr Kott imagines Titania's court to be a gang of slobbering, toothless old men and women – seems imagination run riot, it has at least helped strip layers of romanticism from the play. An age which believed in witches was beginning to doubt fairies. Shakespeare allegedly gave his bunch a good-natured, dreamlike quality. But did he? Mr Kott's view is more in line with pre-Tudor concepts of malign spirits. They are ambivalent creatures in the play and they were in Peter Brook's famous 1970 production.

However, for all the advantages of rethinking a well-loved text which had become taken for granted, it is hard to believe that the traditional view of the play will ever basically alter, for Shakespeare's forest near Athens–Stratford is a place of enchantment. He, surely, was not frightened of spiders or spotted snakes. That is a townsman's fear.

The Merchant of Venice chiefly lives by its great creation, Shylock. He was a villain to the Elizabethans and, whatever the sensitive may say, he remains one despite the humanity of Shakespeare, most notably shown in the 'Hath not a Jew eyes?' speech. Shakespeare, too, makes it clear that it is his daughter's defection and the insults to his race that have made Shylock implacable. He seems more sympathetic because he is surrounded by – for us – unsympathetic Gentile bounders. But Bassanio would probably not have seemed a cad to any Elizabethan, just a young man-about-town running up debts to the manner born, as a gentleman should. Portia, charming and brainy, divides opinion today in a way she presumably did not in Tudor times, because of the way she submits to her husband-to-be in the speech, 'You see me, Lord Bassanio, where I stand'. But she is clearly a match for him, as we see by the end, whatever the Elizabethan code of marriage might say about the conduct of wives. The play has a wide variety of elements – choosing a husband by casket to a pound of flesh is a big jump – but it works. A popular genius makes his own rules.

Henry IV is, as readers may notice, a particular favourite with the author of this book. And with justification. Kenneth Tynan once called the two plays the twin summits of Shakespeare's achievement (when reviewing Douglas Seale's production at the Old Vic in 1955) and wrote of great public plays in which a whole nation is under scrutiny and on trial. The plays are epics which range England as Tamburlaine ranged the known world. They are England, part fourteenth century, part Tudor, and they range from the Court to the battlefield and the countryside. Honour, as has been noted, is a main theme, but so are kingship, friendship, enjoyment and dishonour: Prince John of Lancaster dupes rebels into surrendering and has them executed. Worcester refuses to tell Hotspur of the king's clemency. There are more good parts in the two plays than most major playwrights could manage in thirty plays, not that anyone but Shakespeare could create a Falstaff. Plump Jack is not only witty, but the cause of wit in other men; boastful, bawdy and a reprobate, he has always been adored. He, Shallow, Silence, Wart and Feeble and the rest, not forgetting Doll Tearsheet and Mrs Quickly, are one side of the play, Hotspur, Glendower, Douglas, and Sir Richard Vernon are another, the sleepless king and his courtiers are a third, and Prince Hal, the madcap who is to be an ideal king, is a fourth who links them all. We may revolt against his rejection of Falstaff, but Elizabethans understood it and knew it had to be. These two plays are national glories, England on parade, with all its faults and virtues.

Henry V is less remarkable. Falstaff had to be banished, not only for dramatic and historical reasons, but because nothing must interfere with the Elizabethan vision of King Hal. He dies off-stage, his death incomparably recounted by Mistress Quickly. The play is fascinating because so many points of view are stressed. War is examined closely, and so are its motives. The play has speeches by the Chorus which are rightly regarded as perfection; it has rhetorical, heroic speeches which inspire in times of danger and despair, and thrill all but the most cynical and pacific at other times. It also examines kingship. That it is not as fine a creation as *Henry IV* is beside the point. It is a different sort of play.

As for *The Merry Wives of Windsor*, written, it is said, because the Queen wanted to see Falstaff in love, it is best to treat it as a separate world, for the greatest comic character in English literature is reduced to a butt. The play works in the theatre, it is a fascinating piece of Tudoriana, and for those reasons we can salute it – and pass on.

Page 69   (*above*) David Garrick as Richard III; (*below*) the Play Scene from *Hamlet*

THE CELEBRATED GARRICK JUBILEE AT STRATFORD-ON-AVON, IN THE YEAR 1769.

Page 70 Two glimpses of Garrick's Shakespeare Jubilee in 1769

Julius Caesar is tauter than the English histories. It is a masterly political play with three superb creations: Brutus, Cassius and Mark Antony. That the name part is killed half-way through causes no trouble, for the conspirators rose against Caesarism more than Caesar, and besides, the spirit of Caesar dominates the rest of the play. Strangely, opinions vary widely about Shakespeare's characterisation of Caesar. Some find him noble, others weak and boastful.

So well-known is the most famous scene in the play, the Forum scene, that its extreme brilliance is sometimes taken for granted: Brutus all reason, Antony, emotionally involved, but using craft to create a savage mob which will tear a man to pieces because of his name. Brutus, the noble idealist, is as topical today as ever he was. He refuses to allow Antony to be killed and he allows him to speak in the Forum, despite warnings on both counts by Cassius, who in terms of the struggle for power is utterly right. In a dangerous age it is not enough to be the noblest Roman of them all. Cassius is more complex, for he is flawed by anger, hatred and envy, yet is very human, easily hurt and devoted to Brutus. Antony is a shrewd, high-living romantic. He undoubtedly loved Caesar – his superb speeches tell us so – and if he uses the mob for personal ends as well as vengeance, who can blame him? He has suddenly found himself in a wilderness of tigers. In *Julius Caesar* Shakespeare became the complete professional craftsman and showed a new depth of understanding of human nature, public and private morality, and the meaning of power and justice. Now, with this play and *Henry IV* behind him, he had reached total maturity.

This showed in three great romantic comedies, which spanned the turn of the century, *Much Ado About Nothing*, *As You Like It* and *Twelfth Night*. Charles I put 'Beatrice and Benedick' in his Folio in place of *Much Ado* and who can blame him? Dover Wilson called Beatrice 'the first woman in our literature, perhaps the first in the literature of Europe, who not only had a brain, but delights in the constant employment of it'. Benedick is almost, if not quite, her equal. The main plot functions well enough. The villain, Don John, is driven on by envy, Hero is an appealing wronged heroine, and Claudio, whose suspicious nature triggers off the plot when he suspects Hero of being unfaithful, is notable for his remarkable lack of knowledge of women, his impetuosity, naïvety and obsession with honour. Don Pedro and Leonato are well drawn, while Dogberry, Malapproping away nearly 200 years before that epic figure, is a splendid, daft creature. The play is a most attractive one.

As You Like It, like *Much Ado*, is a 'love-game comedy' (David Stevenson). It is more of a unified whole and richly satisfying, partly because Rosalind is one of Shakespeare's most attractive heroines. Her witty chatter cannot conceal her loving, tender nature. Touchstone, that natural philosopher, has dialogue obscure enough to us today to make him an actor's nightmare, but the right comedian can make him genuinely funny. There are some good small parts, Orlando is a fine straight hero, and Jaques, the play's most original creation, is an odd enough fish to make an audience wonder how an actor is going to play him. He has little effect on the plot and has one of the best-known speeches in all literature, the famous Seven Ages of Man, in which he joylessly and cynically writes us all off from cradle to grave.

Twelfth Night, the finest of the three, is quite simply a masterpiece and an enchantment. The plot is full of stratagems and disguises and twinnish complications resulting from Viola's male disguise which makes her look like her brother Sebastian, but this is all to the good because of the encounters and comic situations that stem from them. Except, perhaps, for Fabian, all the main characters above and below stairs have good parts, and much of the humour survives the centuries, except for Feste's. But he directs events and sings some of the loveliest lyrics ever written, which makes him very welcome.

The play was often called *Malvolio* after its finest creation, Olivia's pompous, puritanical steward, who is made to believe that his mistress loves him. The jovial, tippling Sir Toby asks him an immortal question:

> Dost thou think, because thou art virtuous,
> There shall be no more cakes and ale?

Elizabethans saw Malvolio as a figure of fun and would be surprised that in modern times he sometimes becomes almost a tragic figure at the end. Sir Andrew Aguecheek, his hair hanging down 'like flax on a distaff', is undoubtedly comic. The poor lost creature fears that he may have damaged his wits – they are certainly damaged – because he is a 'great eater of beef'. 'I was adored once', he announces in a rare moment of comic pathos. Viola is the best of the three fine women's parts. She is devoted and loving, and Maria, Olivia's servant, is witty and bright, while Olivia, who has the misfortune to fall in love with Viola disguised as a boy, and Orsino, who is in love with love, can be made much of by the right players. Shakespeare's last romantic comedy has never been surpassed, and those who feel they know it too well rarely fail to succumb from the moment Orsino speaks his familiar opening line – 'If music be the food of love, play on.'

The Dark Comedies that followed, *All's Well that Ends Well*, *Troilus and Cressida* and *Measure for Measure*, are, as F. S. Boas has said, problem plays. *Troilus*, cynical, political, critical of militarism, critical of those who disturb the *status quo*, works best. Thersites sees to it that nobility and honour get short shrift, and Hector alone almost survives with his fame intact. Ulysses is the sanest person in the play, though some have found him a hero and others a villain. Troilus, the romantic young lover, is forced to watch his love, 'false Cressida', betray him. Some say Shakespeare's view of him was ironic, but surely not wholly. A famous speech shows he is no innocent, but it cannot be ironic:

> I am giddy, expectation whirls me round.
> The imaginary relish is so sweet
> That it enchants my sense. What will it be
> When that the watery palate tastes indeed
> Love's thrice-repured nectar?

Shakespeare draws Cressida as a sensuous girl, incapable of being faithful for long to one person, but by no means corrupt. The play is full of interesting parts, none so effective as the deformed, foul-mouthed chorus-like Thersites. He saves himself being killed by a fellow bastard named Margelon by pointing out that they should not 'bite one another' and survives an encounter with the great Hector:

> *Hector*: Art thou for Hector's match?
> Art thou of blood and honour?
> *Thersites*: No, no, I am a rascal; a scurvy railing knave; a very filthy knave.
> *Hector*: I do believe thee: live.

All's Well suffers from a boorish anti-hero, Bertram; its clown,

Lavache, is a gross creature, while Helena, the heroine, is very controversial. Coleridge hailed her as Shakespeare's loveliest character, but
others, noting her methods to get her man, have dubbed her a calculating little opportunist. Isabella in *Measure for Measure* is controversial,
too, for she values her honour more than her brother's life. It is for
the individual to decide whether she is a martyr or a pitiless prig, a
saint or an icicle. Angelo in the same play is a splendidly drawn near-
monster, icy cold and righteous on the outside, inflamed with lust
within. This bawdy, fascinating play is a grim comedy indeed, and
Shakespeare seems to have taken a very pessimistic view of life at the
period he wrote these three studies in corruption.

'Seems' is the operative word, for, without a diary by him, all is
finally conjecture. What is certain is that two of the plays are very
fine and the third, *All's Well*, full of good things, not least the character
of the Countess, the kindly mother of the appalling Bertram and
Helena's guardian. The plays were written at a time of public unease,
with the queen dying, plague rife in the land, and cherished beliefs
being questioned. Shakespeare may have been influenced by these
things, or by private griefs, or both, or neither.

Around the same period, he was writing the most famous of all
plays, *Hamlet*. Its hero has attracted more attention than any other
character in literature. He is the ultimate Renaissance Man in fiction
and 'the expectancy and rose of the fair state', as Ophelia says of him.

A revenge play is the canvas on which Hamlet functions. Endless
arguments rage about every aspect of him, especially his fatal delay
in taking his revenge. So rich and complex is his character that the
part can be played in any number of ways, but however the actor – or
the reader – interprets him, he remains the ultimate Shakespeare Man,
a supreme creation, matchless in his humanity and thought in soliloquy,
prose and much-quoted verse. Is he incapable of accepting the con-
sequence of his destiny? Does his melancholy paralyse him? Is he too
sensitive to seek his revenge? None of the millions of words written
about him ultimately explain his power in the theatre and in the minds
of each generation. Hamlet is every one of us.

In *Hamlet*, Shakespeare's intellectual maturity was as complete as
his dramatic powers. One need look no further than the soliloquies
to recognise this. He surrounded his hero, like a good actor-manager,

with a strong supporting cast: Claudius, sensual, smooth, ambitious and villainous, but showing signs of remorse; Gertrude, weak, easily dominated, also sensual, and by no means unsympathetic; the pathetic Ophelia; her well-meaning father, Polonius, written off by Hamlet as a 'wretched, rash, intruding fool'; his son Laertes, youthful and hot-tempered; Horatio, restrained and loyal to his 'sweet prince'. Best of the small parts is the foppish Osric.

Shakespeare's now total mastery is everywhere apparent from the electric start onwards. After twenty lines, Marcellus asks: 'What! has this thing appear'd again tonight?' and an extra dimension of tension is introduced, culminating in the appearance of the Ghost. Before its second appearance, Horatio is allowed to lower the tension by discussing current affairs when suddenly the Ghost reappears. Hamlet is not mentioned until line 170. Then, in the second scene, we see him in his 'inky cloak', isolated and melancholy. Every scene continues this total mastery.

Unfortunately, the play is too rarely given in its entirety. Some of the supreme plays can have scenes and lines lopped off without a sense of loss, but not *Hamlet*. Now that the repertoire system is more widely used and no actor need be asked to give six to eight Hamlets a week, cuts are inexcusable. Cuts, incidentally, not only affect the play, but allow the actor next to no rest. A complete version gives Hamlet breathing space: Shakespeare naturally was well aware of the need for it.

Othello is less subtle, profound, philosophical and complex than *Hamlet*, partly because the Moor is not given to philosophising. He is a man of action, a leader of men, introduced to us as noble, trusting and proud, but brought down to savagery by the malignant Iago and his own catastrophic jealousy. To some, he is a flawless hero until tragedy overtakes him, to others (most notably T. S. Eliot and F. R. Leavis) he is proud to the point of arrogance, a self-dramatising self-idealist. Cassio, deeply wronged by him, has an answer for these critics who find self-dramatisation even in Othello's last speech, 'I have done the state some service . . .' 'He was great of heart', says Cassio, which is a fine epitaph.

Othello's supreme scene with Iago has already been referred to. Some see Iago as purely evil, others as a personification of the medieval morality character, Vice, and W. H. Auden saw him as a monstrous practical joker. The part is sometimes ruined because the actor makes him too obviously villainous, which turns Othello into a fool even before the green-eyed monster spreads its poison.

Desdemona, for all her innocence, has great character and strength, as well as dignity. When Othello is scourging her with verbal whips, she defends herself courageously:

> *Othello*: Impudent strumpet!
> *Desdemona*: By heaven, you do me wrong.
> *Othello*: Are you not a strumpet?
> *Desdemona*: No, as I am a Christian.
> If to preserve this vessel for my lord
> From any other foul unlawful touch
> Be not to be a strumpet, I am none.
> *Othello*: What! not a whore?
> *Desdemona*: No, as I shall be sav'd.
> *Othello*: Is it possible?
> *Desdemona*: O! heaven forgive us.
> *Othello*: I cry you mercy then;
> I took you for that cunning whore of Venice
> That married with Othello.

There are other fine parts in the play: Cassio, Roderigo, Emilia, all brought down in different ways by venom of Iago. The tragedy is all the greater because we have witnessed the depth of love between the doomed pair. There is a particularly fine moment when we experience this, after the landing in Cyprus by Othello, Desdemona having arrived earlier with Iago. In a moment of calm after the excitement, the bustle and the trumpets, the lovers meet:

> *Othello*: O my fair warrior!
> *Desdemona*: My dear Othello.
> *Othello*: It gives me wonder great as my content
> To see you here before me. O my soul's joy!
> If after every tempest come such calms,
> May the winds blow till they have waken'd death!

> If it were now to die,
> 'Twere now to be most happy, for I fear
> My soul hath her content so absolute
> That not another comfort like to this
> Succeeds in unknown fate.

Othello goes on to speak of 'too much of joy'. Iago is listening. Soon this monstrous manipulator will turn Othello into a tormented, volcanic savage, unique in drama.

Having unleashed such a thunderbolt, Shakespeare wrote *King Lear*. Lear's pride and abdication are totally disastrous to himself and to his country. But it is more than pride. Rage, impulsiveness and foolishness bordering on senility help bring about his downfall and madness. Yet he comes through his ordeal sanely and grandly, supported by those he had despised and driven away – Cordelia, Kent, and Edgar, driven out by *his* foolish father. And Lear has a nobility in misfortune, which had lain dormant, though Kent at least saw Authority in his face.

A titanic figure, when he learns the truth about his she-dragon daughters he threatens them with 'the terrors of the earth', but his speech ends with 'O fool! I shall go mad.'

His road to madness is brilliantly charted, and, as his senses fade, he learns how the unfortunate live. We are prepared for the tragic, pitiful figure of the later scenes. Despite the touching reconciliation with Cordelia, the madness returns at the end. Was this sheer pessimism on Shakespeare's part? Does it mean that evil can be conquered only after death? Dramatically, Cordelia's death could have driven him out of his wits once more, though many believe that he dies thinking she lives. It depends how one interprets the line: 'Look on her, look, her lips, Look there, look there!'

Like characters in a morality play, the good and evil are presented to us in *Lear*, but in a depth quite unknown before. The king has his equivalent in the sub-plot in the foolish Gloucester, who at least learns the truth at the end before his heart 'burst smilingly' – that Edgar, not Edmund, was the loyal son. Edmund is the least appalling of the three main personifications of Evil in the play, for while Goneril and Regan are she-tigresses beyond human feelings except lust and cruelty, he has a flashy charm. 'Now, gods, stand up for bastards!' he exults, and at first they seem to. He is in the Richard III tradition.

Oscar Campbell has characterised Kent, Cordelia and Edgar as Truth, Love and Knowledge, and Cordelia finds a loving husband, while Regan marries a monster. Of the main characters, only the Fool escapes classification. Both jester and commentator, he knows only too well the mistake his beloved master has made in disinheriting Cordelia. Though some have written him off as a simpleton because of his riddles, songs, and morbid jokes, he seems as sensible as he is melancholy. He is a haunting creation.

He vanishes in the middle of the play, which is a good moment to recall Shakespeare, the practical man of the theatre. Some believe that the original Fool may also have acted Cordelia, who is not seen in the middle. This may explain the strange line of Lear's near the end: 'And my poor fool is hanged.'

'Like flies to wanton boys are we to the gods. They kill us for their sport,' says Gloucester, blinded and in despair, at one point in this stupendous play. Its framework is sheer melodramatic Grand Guignol, yet as a study of man's behaviour to man it is the most penetrating of all Shakespeare's plays. And for this searing examination of mankind, he chooses a pagan world, and language, passions and events of epic grandeur.

There followed *Macbeth*, less complex in structure and theme, and with all Shakespeare's imagination and dramatic powers in action to show the progress of a man from ambition to murder, tyranny and eventual ruin and death. Only the Porter provides a moment of comedy, yet he is linked tightly to the plot. As De Quincey noted, he re-establishes the claims of ordinary life after they have been temporarily suspended by the fiendish murder of Duncan, and some have seen him as the guardian of Hell, a throwback to the morality plays. The scenes in England, too, are tightly linked to Macbeth, with Malcolm being shown as fit to rule; with the depths of Macbeth's villainy (the murder of the family of Macduff) being revealed; and the need for ridding a nation of its king being rammed home. The Witches, too, are essential to the plot except when Hecate leads them in a song and dance, which was a later insertion by another writer.

Macbeth, amazingly, is a villain who is also a tragic hero. His loyalty and nobility are eroded by ambition until he is reduced to blackest pessimism and despair and total moral collapse. But the verse of this soldier poet grows more impressive as his crimes multiply. Finally, he has 'supp'd full with horrors' and 'almost forgot the taste of fears'. He reaches a nadir of bleak, stoical pessimism where life is 'a tale told by an idiot, full of sound and fury, signifying nothing'. He goes down like a tiger.

Lady Macbeth banished her womanhood and all pity to get her husband on the throne. Her nerve is better than his, and her will stronger, but even this cold villainess is overtaken by conscience, for in her great sleepwalking scene she tries to wash away the blood she thinks is on her hands. Her total dedication to Macbeth and the remorse below her steely exterior make the part great. Though the play is by no means a two-hander, its greatness is concentrated in the two, and the title-role is one of the hardest in which to succeed fully that Shakespeare ever wrote. Put at its most simple, it is hard to find an actor ideally cast as a man who is both soldier and poet.

Antony and Cleopatra divides opinion. For some, because of the golden, incomparable splendour of the verse it is the supreme tragedy, or, at least, the equal of the other four. Others (profoundly to be pitied) find the verse too rich to the point of cloying. The theme is simple enough, love or duty, the duty here being an empire, a world. This is a chronicle play transformed into a stupendous love duet and love duel, supreme in art and approached only by Wagner in *Tristan and Isolde*. The comparison is apt, for Cleopatra's matchless speeches about her dead Antony have a magnificence which links them to Isolde's *Liebestod* (love death). Both welcome death, for it will redeem them and they will be reunited with their loves.

For all the difficulty of finding an actress to play Cleopatra, Antony is the more difficult part, not least because this 'triple pillar of the world' turned into a 'strumpet's fool' is constantly praised, especially by Cleopatra, in superhuman terms but is rarely seen justifying it. We get a glimpse of his noble nature when Enobarbus has betrayed him and Antony still is able to send his 'treasure' to him, but that is all. Except for one all-transfiguring thing, the verse. For the play's worshippers, there is no problem with Antony. We believe what is said about him.

Cleopatra is capricious to a degree, frank, funny, fascinating, sensual and clever, hot-tempered and passionate. We watch and hear her 'infinite variety'. Her woman Charmian sums her up in the greatest epitaph in literature, supreme because of the last two words quoted here, which are beyond comment:

> Now boast thee, death, in thy possession lies
> A lass unparallel'd.

The play is full of finely drawn characters, most notably Enobarbus, eloquent, witty, likeable, but finally false, and Octavius, cold, calculating and ruthless, power politics made human, but without humanity. At the play's end he officially laments 'a pair so famous'. He can afford to: he owns the world.

To sum up, either Shakespeare was intending a detached view of the dangers of passion, or he was celebrating its power to overcome even death. Shakespeare, gentleman of Stratford, was no Antony, for all his own mysterious sexual adventures. He disliked those who disturbed the *status quo*. But surely he responded to Antony (and Essex). Like many quiet people, he was charmed by attractive men of action almost to the point of hero-worship, though he knew that leaders like the pragmatic Octavius Caesar of the play make better rulers. The verse of *Antony* gives the game away. Shakespeare knew the faults of his lovers but he gave his heart to them.

His next leading characters are so flawed that to call them heroes would be stretching the word beyond its meaning. This is especially so of the name part in *Timon of Athens*. Timon, at first the most magnanimous of men – to the point of foolishness – loses his fortunes, is deserted by his so-called friends, and is transformed into the most spectacular misanthrope in drama. He has a superb line in invective:

> Maid, to thy master's bed;
> Thy mistress is o' the brothel! Son of sixteen,
> Pluck the lin'd crutch from thy old limping sire,
> With it beat out his brains! Piety, and fear,
> Religion to the gods, peace, justice, truth,
> Domestic awe, night-rest and neighbourhood,
> Instruction, manners, mysteries and trades,
> Degrees, observances, customs and laws,
> Decline to your confounding contraries,

> And let confusion live! Plagues incident to men,
> Your potent and infectious fevers heap
> On Athens, ripe for stroke! Thou cold sciatica,
> Cripple our senators, that their limbs may halt
> As lamely as their manners.

He goes on to wish itches, blains and bad breath on all and sundry; vigorous words, but in later scenes the same tune is played until the effect is lessened unless a very remarkable actor is playing the part.

Regarded as tragedy, the play is something of a failure, but as a tragic satire it makes sense. Even at his least successful, Shakespeare is intensely interesting, especially at this time in his career, but that is all one can truly say about *Timon*.

Coriolanus is a much finer play. The anti-hero is graceless, snobbish (a trait he picks up from Volumnia, his alarming mother) and proud beyond safety limits, and it is this last quality which brings him down. He despises his soldiers and (with some justification) his demagogic enemies, the tribunes of Rome, and he has no time for the people. Patience and self-control are unknown virtues to him and when his Volscian enemy, Tullus Aufidius, calls him 'Thou boy of tears', the stinging comment on his immaturity is just.

Yet there is nobility, not just bravery, in Coriolanus, which must come out in performance. His overpowering mother is to blame for much about him, but he has a true friend in Menenius Agrippa, a wise Tory patrician. His contempt for the populace is so blatant that it is just as well his enemies are so unlikeable. It is hard to find Shakespeare's attitude, except on the order versus chaos issue, for as so often he is neutral and therefore able once again to present a wide range of people as they really are.

Poetry is lacking in the play, but when it comes it is thrilling:

> I tell you he does sit in gold, his eye
> Red as 'twould burn Rome.

and

> then let the mutinous winds
> Strike the proud cedars gainst the fiery sun.

81

These are spoken by Cominius and Coriolanus respectively, but much of the finest writing is searing prose, some of it as fine as anything Shakespeare wrote elsewhere; for instance, 'the tartness of his face sours ripe grapes'. Sometimes Coriolanus reaches heights of invective that Timon would envy:

> You common cry of curs! whose breath I hate
> As reek o' the rotten fens, whose loves I prize
> As the dead carcasses of unburied men
> That do corrupt my air, I banish you.

His death scene is thrilling. After Aufidius has insulted him as a boy of tears, he cries:

> Measureless liar, thou hast made my heart
> Too great for what contains it.

And when he is dead, Aufidius repents nobly:

> My rage is gone,
> And I am struck with sorrow.

Perhaps one of the strengths of this remarkable play is that it is always topical. It is certainly always welcome.

The 'Romances' that followed, *Pericles, Cymbeline, The Winter's Tale* and *The Tempest*, were presumably written primarily for the Blackfriars. *Pericles* is an unsubtle play full of sensational incidents – pirates, a fire from heaven, etc – and strange events, while the sorely tried hero ranges the seas until he finds peace at the last after enduring afflictions on a Job-like scale. The low scenes are superb, especially the complications that ensue when Marina, the innocent young heroine, practically bankrupts the brothel into which she is put by her radiant goodness. The poor Pandar finds her reforming the customers. The medieval poet, John Gower, is enlisted by Shakespeare to act as Chorus to this mixture of fairy-tale, musical and drama and bawdy comedy, for Gower himself re-told the tale from the Latin. It is an odd, likeable piece.

Cymbeline is equally action-packed, with many features of the masque, including the stage direction: 'Jupiter descends in thunder and lightning, sitting upon an eagle: he throws a thunderbolt. The Ghosts fall on their knees.' The play found Shakespeare experimenting with the new 'romantic' genre for the Blackfriars' audience and, if it is not altogether successful, there is no reason to find 'another hand' at work. Two characters, the enchanting Imogen and the wicked Iachimo, are major creations; 'Hark! hark! the lark' is a lovely song and 'Fear no more the heat o' the sun' is incomparable. If the several plots are not linked as well as usual, if, perhaps, the play shows signs of being a pot-boiler at times, Shakespeare could still assemble eight surprises in the last scene and, overall, produce an enchanting play. Tennyson had a copy buried with him.

The Winter's Tale needs no apologies. There are plenty of sensations and surprises, but the playwright was at pains to make everything credible within the setting of a Romance. He took risks, but created characters strong enough to bear them. Leontes's devastating jealousy, which triggers off the plot, and which leaves his wife Hermione apparently dead, their son dead, and their daughter abandoned on the coast of Bohemia, suggests mental illness and weakness of character, but is believable. Hermione and Paulina are beautifully drawn, while in the pastoral fourth act, spring instead of previous winter, and set sixteen years later, we meet the abandoned child, now grown into Perdita, the ideal girl heroine of romance. Her lover Florizel says of her:

> . . . when you do dance, I wish you
> A wave o' the sea, that you might ever do
> Nothing but that.

In this pastoral world, part dream, part Warwickshire, we also meet Autolycus, a pedlar and rogue and Elizabethan spiv, whose songs include 'When daffodils begin to peer'. Later, back at court, it is high summer, for Hermione 'magically' comes back to life and all the complications are sorted out. Superlatives are the bane of books on Shakespeare, but, without apologies, it can be said that this is a most wonderful and beautiful play.

The last of the plays written entirely by Shakespeare was *The Tempest*. It is the most famous of the Romances, but, unlike the rest, is not so full of action and surprises. Like the play, the leading character, Prospero, divides opinion. His magic powers were yet another extension of Shakespeare's own powers, but not everyone responds to him. For all his magnificent verse, some find him too all-knowing, too powerful, like an omniscient headmaster. Yet he grows in humanity and nobly forgives his enemies at the end.

Some see *The Tempest* as the culmination of Shakespeare's art, others as an allegory of his life. Like all his greatest work it can survive extremes of interpretation, but the idea that Shakespeare can be found in Prospero's invocation of magic collapses in the face of some lines which would make him – in front of an audience – very boastful indeed. Prospero's potent art has 'bedimm'd The noontide sun, called forth the mutinous winds'. It cannot be too much stressed that part of Shakespeare's genius was his ability to stand outside his characters, and his neutrality must never be forgotten. Yet that neutrality is never negative. In this last play, the deformed brutish Caliban (an anagram of can[n]ibal) typifies this aspect of his genius. It was to the monster that Shakespeare gave this speech:

> Be not afeard: the isle is full of noises,
> Sounds and sweet airs, that give delight, and hurt not.
> Sometimes a thousand twangling instruments
> Will hum about mine ears; and sometimes voices,
> That, if I then had wak'd after long sleep,
> Will make me sleep again: and then, in dreaming,
> The clouds methought would open and show riches
> Ready to drop upon me; that when I wak'd
> I cried to dream again.

After *The Tempest*, Shakespeare seems to have collaborated with John Fletcher on at least three occasions, *Henry VIII, The Two Noble Kinsmen* and *Cardenio*. This book is concerned only with plays in the First Folio and *Pericles*, so only *Henry VIII*, the finest parts of it by Shakespeare, so experts say, is up for consideration. Wolsey, Queen Katharine and to some extent Henry are the characters who live. Let it be noted how Shakespeare in Protestant England made Katharine a very sympathetic person. Apart from them the most vivid creations are the smallest fry, like the Porter and his Man, who appear before the infant Elizabeth's christening. This scene has one of the only pieces of bawdy in the play, and, as A. L. Rowse has pointed out, 'the old hand has not lost its cunning'. It is even topical, with America in the news when the play was written (though not in Henry's time). Says the Porter: '. . . or have we some strange Indian with the great tool come to court, the women so besiege us? Bless me, what a fry of fornication is at the door! On my Christian conscience, this one christening will beget a thousand.'

The play is not planned like the earlier, greater chronicles, which examine kingship, the rise and fall of kings and commoners. It is a splendid pageant play, a sort of historical masque for the populace who flocked to the Globe. It has an epilogue of considerable charm, which disarmingly states that ' 'Tis ten to one this play can never please All that are here: some come to take their ease And sleep an act or two . . .' What little we know about how much this and the other plays pleased is the subject of the next chapter.

4

AS THEY LIKED IT

. . . let but Falstaffe *come,*
Hall, Poines, *the rest you scarce shall have a roome*
All is so pester'd . . . – Leonard Digges

'Though God hath raised me high, yet this I count the glory of my crown: that I have reigned with your loves.'

So spoke Gloriana in her Golden Speech of 1601 around the time that her greatest subject, as we now confidently assert, was writing *Hamlet*. Yet in his own day Shakespeare was one star among many, not even an Everest in the Himalayas, still less a mountain rising sheer from foothills as he is today.

Contemporary references indicate his early rating among critics. 'Gentle' in person, his art was 'sweet' and 'honey-tongued'. Ben Jonson's noble tribute, recognising that he was not of an age but for all time, was a salute from a genius to one greater than himself. Shakespeare might – so Jonson alleged – break the rules and lack art, but Jonson never doubted his friend and rival's universality.

On evidence, few others were so optimistic. The public, however, continued to flock to Shakespeare's plays after his death. They were so popular that Leonard Digges could write, 'by him the King's men live'. Digges, in the same poem, printed in 1640 five years after his own death, also wrote of Shakespeare's 'art unparaleld'. And John Hales, an anti-Puritan divine of Eton, refused to allow Shakespeare's ignorance. As for the Friendly Admirer, in a poem prefacing the Second Folio of 1632 this unknown but very talented author wrote of 'A Mind reflecting ages past' and how 'time shall never stain, nor envy tear' the plays.

Milton was a great admirer of 'sweetest Shakespeare, Fancy's child',

Page 87   (*above*) The Royal Shakespeare Theatre, Stratford-upon-Avon;
(*below*) The Festival Theatre, Stratford, Ontario

Page 88   Laurence Olivier as Othello at the National Theatre, 1964

Marlon Brando as Mark Antony in Joseph Mankiewicz's film of *Julius Caesar*, 1953

and Dryden, the first major Shakespearean critic, hailed him as divine, but noted the lack of art.

Dryden apart, the Restoration period saw Shakespeare's reputation at its lowest, with 'improvements' made to a number of the plays to satisfy the so-sophisticated tastes of the day, and with one Thomas Rymer, the worst type of orthodox academic, informing the world that Othello is a 'bloody farce without salt or savour' and that Caesar and Brutus were above the playwright's conversation, in other words, he had never met such superior people and had no idea how they talked or behaved. Thanks to some actors and audiences, and to his own indestructibility, Shakespeare survived such rubbish and a dismal period.

In the eighteenth century things improved. Art was still considered to be lacking, but genius was recognised. The great Doctor Johnson belaboured Voltaire and his 'Shakespeare the Barbarian' cult and, though he found plenty of faults with the author and his worshippers, wrote finely of his skill in creating 'human sentiments or human actions'. He was fascinated by Shakespeare's characters, as are all Shakespeareans except the extreme fringe of imagery-obsessed scholars whom we met in the last chapter.

It was the Romantic age which saw the final breakthrough. Coleridge hailed Shakespeare as the supreme artist and came out with the (then) sensational statement – 'Shakespeare's Judgement Equal to his Genius'. This was the title of one of his two very influential essays on Shakespeare. He even refuted Johnson's allegations of moral and verbal grossness. Lamb also hailed Shakespeare, as did Hazlitt, for whom he was the greatest, most universal genius who ever lived. It is interesting that Coleridge and Hazlitt both experienced the electric performances of the most exciting of all English actors, Edmund Kean, and wrote thrillingly about him.

Since that time Shakespearean criticism has grown into a major field of scholarship; but whatever disputes arise over individual plays, characters, lines, speeches or ideas, his position is unassailable. It is not that he is beyond criticism – the speed at which he worked and the fact that he was human ensure plenty of scope for argument – but that his plays are the pinnacle of art. There is no arrogance in his awe-inspiring eminence, unlike his own Richard III, who could say: '. . . I was born so high, Our aery buildeth in the cedar's top, And dallies with the wind, and scorns the sun'. Rather there is the supremacy which Théophile Silvestre attributed to Delacroix:

> There was a sun in his head and storms in his heart who for forty years had played upon the keyboard of human passions, and whose brush, grandiose, terrible and suave, passed from saints to warriors, from warriors to lovers, from lovers to tigers and from tigers to flowers.

The industry that has grown up round Shakespeare belongs to Chapter 6. Here, we must now consider the frustratingly small evidence of his popularity in his own day. It is frustrating only because of the gaps in our knowledge, for of his success there can be no doubt. There was the material success which led to Will Shakespeare, Gent, of Stratford, and there was the popularity of which Leonard Digges and others speak. The quotations are all vital and there are many contemporary references to public and private performances. But there was no *Who's Who in the Theatre* in Shakespeare's day, which makes it impossible to be sure just how many hits Shakespeare wrote. The Rose Theatre had Henslowe to keep a diary of events, but if there was such a diary at the Globe it has vanished. The fact that a repertoire of plays was always given – no runs, long or short – makes the task still harder. We are left with a number of allusions to performances, a number of records of plays given at Court or in other special surroundings, and the evidence of the texts published in Shakespeare's lifetime. Some of them were pirated and 'bad', like the *Romeo* of 1596 and the *Hamlet* of 1603, but that is significant: no one would bother to scribble down an unpopular text.

Going through the plays in the order chosen in the last chapter, we begin with *The Comedy of Errors* and *Titus Andronicus*. The first, written around 1592, is known to have been given at Gray's Inn in December 1594 in front of a legal audience and played ten years later to the day at Court. At the very least this proves that it stayed in the repertoire, though it never achieved a Quarto, unlike the shocker shot through with occasional glory, *Titus Andronicus*. This was a hit, presumably because of the amount of bloodshed and the children baked in the pie, and it achieved three Quartos, two of which mentioned 'sundry performances by the Lord Chamberlain's Men'.

Around the same period came *Henry VI*. None of the three plays was mentioned by Francis Meres in his 1598 list, but we know that Part 1 was hugely popular if, as many assume, it was the *Harey the vj* that Henslowe mentioned in 1592. Strange's Men had a colossal hit on their hands, the gallery taking an all-time record of 1,840 pence at its première. There were fourteen performances in three months, sometimes in front of an alleged 10,000 people. The hero, 'brave Talbot', was a particular favourite. Parts 2 and 3 got respectively a bad Quarto and a bad Octavo in 1594 and 1595, but there are no records of performances to help assess their popularity. Only in our own time have the plays come into their own, in the 1950s thanks to Birmingham Rep, in the 1960s at Stratford as part of the brilliant Peter Hall/John Barton *Wars of the Roses*.

Richard III, written by 1593, was a winner, as it is to this day. It had six Quartos by 1622, was Burbage's first great triumph, and was played at Court in 1633. Apart from an odd gap in Restoration times, it has always held the stage, though from 1700 to 1821 the version of the actor-manager-playwright Colley Cibber was used. It had at least one very good extra line – 'Off with his head. So much for Buckingham.' The three most famous Richards have been Garrick, Edmund Kean and Olivier.

The Taming of the Shrew, written around the same time, was not printed until the First Folio. It had been given by the Lord Chamberlain's Men at Newington Butts in 1594 and was played at Court in 1633, so it clearly stayed in the repertoire. Mangled in the Restoration period, it was not properly given until the 1840s. Then Benjamin Webster not only restored the text, but had J. R. Planché stage it at the Haymarket minus spectacular scenery, indeed with so little scenery that the production ranks as a landmark in the struggle to recover the speed and simplicity of Elizabethan staging.

The Two Gentlemen of Verona was first published in the First Folio. Written around the same time as the *Shrew*, it had never been very popular, and is not known to have been performed until the eighteenth century. It goes better in Europe than in Britain.

As we have seen, the closing of the theatres because of plague gave Shakespeare a chance to establish himself as a poet. *Venus and Adonis*, published in 1593, sped through ten editions in ten years. In the play

The Return from Parnassus, published in 1606 anonymously, a foolish undergraduate exults: 'I'll worship sweet Mr Shakespeare, and to honour him will lay his *Venus and Adonis* under my pillow.' Though the passage was satirical, it reflects the delight of the poem's cultivated readers at the time.

The Rape of Lucrece, published in 1594 and reprinted seven times by 1640, was almost as popular and, being less erotic, was presumably welcomed more by staider readers. Gabriel Harvey's comment that the 'younger sort' delighted in *Venus* but the 'wiser sort' in *Lucrece* and *Hamlet* reflects something of this.

The Sonnets, though not printed until 1609, were known to Shakespeare's friends and acquaintances long before. These 'sugared' poems, as Meres called them, were not reprinted until 1640, which is strange enough to make it possible that their contents caused some scandal when they were printed. Unlike the first two poems, the popularity of the finest and most accessible of the sonnets has never waned.

Love's Labour's Lost (1593–4) seems to have been popular with Court and aristocratic audiences for whom it was probably written. The Queen saw it in 1597 and its one reliable Quarto dates from the following year. Despite its wealth of topical allusions and private jokes, and its apparent disappearance from the stage until the nineteenth century, it has had a number of popular productions in modern times, the most magical being Peter Brook's at Stratford in 1946.

King John (1596–7), despite Burbage as the magnificent Bastard, appears to have been unsuccessful. Its first recorded performance was in 1737, and there is no Quarto. It got a mention from Francis Meres and was possibly at its most popular in the nineteenth century because of the ample scope for spectacle. It is still seen from time to time. The most notorious production was by Beerbohm Tree, who put in a dumb-show Magna Carta, which Shakespeare had inconveniently left out.

Richard II has been far more popular. Six Quartos appeared between 1597 and 1634, and though it was considered 'so old and out of use' when the Essex supporters asked for a performance, as described earlier (page 46), must have swung back rapidly into favour once James I came to the throne. Its history includes a ship's performance aboard the *Dragon* off Sierra Leone in 1607, given by members of the crew. Though it was played in the eighteenth century, its modern popularity dates from Charles Kean's very elaborate 1857 production. The most famous modern Richards have been Frank Benson and Gielgud.

Romeo and Juliet, written, like *Richard*, around 1595, was a hit on the evidence of its first Quarto (there were to be four), for by 1597 it had 'been often (with great applause) plaid publiquely'. The Bodleian's copy of the First Folio is more crumpled at the page where the lovers bid each other farewell after their wedding night than anywhere else in the book. To the eternal shame of the Restoration theatre's taste, the play was altered to end happily. It has always been loved by audiences. Even in a book not greatly concerned with famous performances, two in this play cannot be left out: Peggy Ashcroft's Juliet and Edith Evans's Nurse. The latter spanned thirty-five years and was described by W. A. Darlington as being 'as earthy as a potato, as slow as a cart-horse, and as cunning as a badger'.

A Midsummer Night's Dream, which dates from the same period, was another success in its day, as the Quarto of 1600 reveals. Pepys thought the play the most insipid and ridiculous he had ever seen, and soon it was transformed into the operatic spectacular, *The Fairy Queen*, which at least involved a genius, Henry Purcell. Not until 1840 was it given almost as written by Charles Mathews and Elizabeth Vestris, then Samuel Phelps at the Wells gave the play as enchantingly as it was complete. Greatly loved ever since, milestones in its modern history have been Beerbohm Tree's live rabbits in 1901, Peter Brook's famous production of 1970, which has toured the world, and Benjamin Britten's truly Shakespearean opera.

The Merchant of Venice, written between 1596 and 1598, was a success in its own time, with four Quartos, then was neglected during the Restoration period. It has never ceased to be a favourite from the moment in 1741 when Charles Macklin played 'the Jew that Shakespeare drew'. It was as Shylock that Edmund Kean made his name in London, and the part was one of Irving's greatest. Critics have railed against the plot from time to time and some have fatuously dubbed the playwright a racialist. Playgoers very sensibly take no notice and enjoy the play.

In 1596 or 1597, Elizabethan playgoers first delightedly met their adored Sir John Falstaff in *Henry IV Part 1*. The play had gone through eight Quartos by 1639, with Hotspur and Prince Hal helping pack the theatres. Part 2 must surely have been popular, but not as much as the first play. Only one Quarto must be regarded as proof, though that speaks of 'sundrie' performances. There were three Quartos of *The Merry Wives of Windsor*, which both James I and Charles I saw. This lesser play, which acts better than it reads, has been often revived. The true Falstaff plays – Part 1 even pleased Pepys – have fortunately been seen quite often, though never enough for their admirers. The most famous Falstaff of our times has been Ralph Richardson, the most famous Hotspur, Olivier, both in the historic Old Vic production at the New (1945–6).

There followed *Henry V*, first performed in 1599, with Burbage as Tudor England's darling. There were three Quartos, then the play was banished in Restoration times in favour of Lord Orrery's *Henry V*, a noble piece according to Pepys. The eighteenth century saw Shakespeare doctored by Aaron Hill, the nineteenth century wanted and got spectacle, while in 1900 Benson leapt over the walls of Harfleur in full armour. Lewis Waller, complete with trumpet-toned voice, had audiences cheering in World War I, since when the climate of the times has sometimes affected productions. Olivier in his magnificent wartime film gave the play as written, while Stratford in the 1960s deliberately played down the heroic, rhetorical side of the play, in keeping with anti-war sentiment.

Julius Caesar was first performed in 1599 and its popularity was noted by Digges. Its drawing-power lasted until the theatres were closed and at the Restoration it escaped the usual butchery, partly because it was in the repertoire of the King's Company, not Davenant's. A performance in 1671 had Charles Hart – possibly Shakespeare's grandnephew – as Brutus. Only in the late nineteenth century did the play get slightly neglected, and an additional claim to fame is that it is a perfect and much-used way to introduce schoolboys to Shakespeare by acting and reading him in the classroom.

Much Ado About Nothing (*c*1598) was a hit, Digges picking out Beatrice and Benedick as the house-fillers. Alas, the Restoration sank to new depths of theatrical infamy when Davenant put them into a version of *Measure for Measure*. However, the eighteenth century made amends, and from Garrick's day the play has been a favourite, for exactly the same reasons that Digges mentioned.

As You Like It, written around 1599, has no Quarto. Can it be that Touchstone was too much even for the Elizabethans? Hardly. It was registered in 1600 to prevent a pirated edition, which suggests popularity. And if it was played at Wilton (see p 47) that is another reason for thinking it was liked, if not as much as some of the comedies. Since the mid-eighteenth century, and despite its having been continually set for exams, it has been popular enough for continual revivals to be staged, surely Rosalind being the play's greatest attraction.

The third of this group of comedies is *Twelfth Night*, written again around 1599. We have Digges's word for it that it was a theatre-filler, Malvolio being an especial attraction. Pepys thought it silly, and a wretched Oxford-educated lawyer named Burnaby went beyond mere thoughts and produced a horrible travesty of the play in 1703 called *Love Betrayed or The Agreeable Disappointment*. Malvolio and Sir Andrew became one (his name was Taquilet) and Maria was cut into two. Since Garrick's day, the play's position has never been in question, not least because it has three superb parts for actresses.

Of the three Dark Comedies, *All's Well that Ends Well* (c1602), *Troilus and Cressida* (c1601) and *Measure for Measure* (c1603), only *Troilus* rated a Quarto (1609), which stated that it had been acted at the Globe. *Measure for Measure* was given at Court in 1604, while *All's Well* is first known to have been played in 1741. Today, partly because of the Royal Shakespeare Company, partly owing to its cynical, anti-war attitudes and to its fascinating characters, *Troilus* is almost a popular play. *Measure for Measure* gets fairly regular productions, partly because the part of Angelo attracts major actors, while *All's Well* is sometimes given.

Hamlet, published in 1603, the first of five Quartos, and written some two years earlier, was a very palpable hit from the first, with Burbage as the Prince and Shakespeare (perhaps) as the Ghost. The Quarto noted performances at Oxford and Cambridge as well as in London. The earliest recorded performance was aboard that most theatrically inclined ship, the *Dragon*, off Sierra Leone in 1607. Charles I saw it in 1637 at Hampton Court, and millions have seen it since. In modern times the most famous American Hamlet was John Barrymore, the most famous British one, Gielgud. Davenant's butchery of the play was less dedicated than usual, omissions taking the place of distortions, and Pepys adored the great Thomas Betterton in the title role. Betterton was then twenty-six and he was still playing the part almost fifty years later.

Othello, written almost certainly in 1604, did not get printed until 1622, but seems to have been continuously popular, being given at the Globe, the Blackfriars and at Court. Digges noted that honest Iago and the jealous Moor were more to the public's taste than Ben Jonson's tragedies and the play survived the Restoration by being given by the King's Company, not Davenant's. It was in *Othello* that a professional actress first appeared on the English stage. The King's Company played it at Thomas Killigrew's Vere Street Theatre on 8 December 1660, and the actress may have been Margaret Hughes. The noble line of *great* Othellos is a short one. It includes Kean, Edwin Forrest, Salvini and Olivier.

King Lear, written between 1605 and 1606, and performed at Court in 1606, had its first of three Quartos two years later. It seems to have been popular and was revived, fairly truthfully it is believed, by Betterton. But in 1681 it was mightily abused by Nahum Tate, who supplied a happy ending which was kept until 1838. The play's saviour was William Macready, a near-great or great actor who despised his profession but did the stage some service. Despite Charles Lamb's claim that 'the Lear of Shakespeare cannot be acted', there have been plenty of actors ready to dispute him, most notably Donald Wolfit in Britain and Morris Carnovsky in the United States.

Macbeth, prone to ill-luck backstage and on-stage, and certainly not to be quoted anywhere in a theatre except on stage in rehearsal or performance, was written in 1605–6 and almost certainly much enjoyed by James I. Being a witch buff, the play was a must for him, and an added attraction was the appearance of Banquo, his (actually mythical) ancestor. Simon Forman saw the play at the Globe in 1611. Davenant excelled himself with his all-singing, all-dancing, all-action version, with its 'new clothes, new scenes, machines, as flyings for the witches'.

David Garrick brought back the play 'as written by Shakespeare', but allowed the popular song-and-dance witches to remain and would not restore the Porter. And he wrote a dying speech for the hero. Kean and Macready removed many of the distortions that still remained and Samuel Phelps, in 1847, finally removed the last traces of the Davenant era. Charles Kean promptly brought them back. Since then, Shakespeare's *Macbeth* has been given, though finding a worthy hero for the name part has always proved difficult. Perhaps Olivier in 1955 came nearest to it in modern times, while the most famous Lady Macbeth in theatre history was the stupendous Sarah Siddons.

Antony and Cleopatra, written in 1606-7, is not thought to have been very popular in Shakespeare's day, perhaps because tastes had changed and grand tragedy was less admired. It was published in the First Folio, and a document of 1669 mentions that it had been performed at the Blackfriars. Dryden's *All for Love* supplanted it in 1678, and for a century, and in Victorian times realistic scenery hampered a play with forty-two scenes. Robert Atkins's Old Vic production in 1922, with next to no scenery and only one curtain drop, ushered in a new era, but even now, partly because of the extreme difficulty of casting the principals, the masterpiece is all too rarely seen. Amazingly, at the time of writing in 1973, London has two productions, one very finely done at the Aldwych (and at Stratford in 1972) with Richard Johnson and Janet Suzman, directed by Trevor Nunn, another at Sam Wanamaker's Globe on Bankside, which strives to be 'different' to a remarkable degree – and is. The most famous production and performances in modern times were at Stratford in 1953, with Michael Redgrave and Peggy Ashcroft, directed by Glen Byam Shaw.

There has been a history of bad Cleopatras. Tallulah Bankhead barged down the Nile and sank according to legend, though John Mason Brown's famous review had her barging down the aisle and sinking. A Russian comedienne named Eugenie Leontovich was quite unintelligible in London in 1936, moving Charles Morgan to write a phonetic version of one great speech in *The Times*. Instead of:

> O, withered is the garland of the war,
> The soldier's pole is fall'n: young boys and girls
> Are level now with men.

the audience heard:

> O weederdee degarlano devar
> Desolderpo lees falln: yong boisenguls
> Alefelnow wimen.

97

On another occasion a royal mistress played the royal mistress of old Egypt, but the mistress's self-inspired idea failed because dramatically she had not got what it takes. Her name was Lily Langtry.

Timon of Athens (*c*1605), fascinating as it is, has never been popular, but *Coriolanus* (1607–8), for all its apparent lack of success in Jacobean times, has gradually established itself and is now a play to which many Shakespeareans always eagerly look forward. Nahum Tate did a terrible piece of surgery on the play in 1681 with his *The Ingratitude of the Common-Wealth*, and others got into the tasteless act. None could equal Tate, though. He incorporated the attempted rape of Virgilia and her suicide and a stark-mad Volumnia going berserk over her grandson's tortured but not-yet-dead body, along with other horrors in both senses of the word. From the mid-eighteenth century Shakespeare was restored, and the most famous performances in the play have included Siddons as Volumnia, and Macready and Olivier and (in America) Edwin Forrest as Coriolanus.

There followed the four Romances, *Pericles*, *Cymbeline*, *The Winter's Tale* and *The Tempest*. *Pericles* (1608–9), so rarely performed in our times, was a tremendous success in Shakespeare's day, with six Quartos between 1609 and 1635. Records of performances include one in front of the French Ambassador in 1619. 'In the King's greate chamber they went to see the play of *Pirracles* Prince of Tyre, which lasted till two a clocke.' Its popularity annoyed Jonson who, after the failure of his *New Inn*, criticised audiences for liking 'some mouldy tale, Like *Pericles*' better. No masterpiece, it needs a good director today, but does not deserve the over-production it normally gets.

Cymbeline was 'well-liked' by Charles I in 1634. Written around 1609–10, it is so full of good things that its appearances are always welcomed. It had no Quartos and was ousted by *The Injured Princess or The Fatal Wager* by Thomas D'Urfey in Restoration times. Since then it has appeared at irregular intervals, the marvellous parts of Imogen and Iachimo helping to ensure that actors liked it. Famous Imogens have included Ellen Terry, Peggy Ashcroft and Vanessa Redgrave.

The Winter's Tale, written in 1611 or, possibly, the year before, was regularly performed at Court, and Simon Forman saw it at the Globe in 1611. It appears to have vanished until 1741, after which abbreviated versions concentrating on Perdita and Florizel were given. The nineteenth century saw Shakespeare's play on the stage again, since when it has been fairly regularly revived, not least because of its wealth of good acting parts. Famous performances have included Mary Anderson as Perdita and Hermione, Ellen Terry (who first spoke on stage as Mamillius) as Hermione, and Gielgud as Leontes in Peter Brook's magical production of 1951.

As for *The Tempest* (1611–12), it was given at Court in 1611 and, later, totally altered by Davenant. His *The Tempest, or The Enchanted Island* is pleasant enough and has music by Purcell. It has been seen at the Old Vic in the 1950s and, despite extra characters like Sycorax, sister of Caliban, can be enjoyed on its own merits, even though it is an artistic atrocity. Dryden was also involved. Not until 1838 was the original play given after other adventures had befallen it since Davenant's time. Some of it disappeared again in 1857 when Charles Kean gave it, because the scenic effects took up so much time, and needed 'the aid of 140 operatives' to work them. In this century it has been frequently revived.

Henry VIII, after its fiery baptism in 1613, has been given fairly frequently, not least at coronation times. The Restoration and, in particular, William Davenant having taken some hard knocks – rightly – in this chapter, it is pleasant to note that when Thomas Betterton played Henry he was coached by Davenant 'from what he had heard from old Mr. Lowen [John Lowin] that had his instructions from Mr. Shakespear himself'. Lowin lived to see the closing of the theatres.

Not much has been made of this tragic event in this book because (mercifully) it happened long after Shakespeare's death, but it is worth recalling the misery it entailed, the sudden abolition of a fine profession. Many of the younger actors fought naturally enough for the King; some seem to have managed to give the occasional secret performance. But the older men who knew Shakespeare must have endured much misery, even if their circumstances were reasonable. It is sad to think that one of Shakespeare's band of brothers, John Lowin, born the son of a carpenter in 1576, having enjoyed a long and honourable career, was 'superannuated' when the Civil War broke out, and 'in his latter days kept an inn (the Three Pigeons) at Brentford, where he dyed very old (for he was an actor of eminent note in the reign of King James the First), and his poverty was as great as his age.' So wrote the theatre historian, James Wright, who was born in 1643. He recalled that Lowin was acting at the Cockpit when troops raided the theatre. Actors rightly lament their uncertain lot today, as they have for centuries, but at least none suffered the fate of Lowin, a Falstaff who knew Shakespeare, and others like him, who were subjected to theatrical genocide. When he died his friends could truly have said: 'Fear no more the frown o' the great, Thou art past the tyrant's stroke.' Perhaps one of them also quoted the last line of that noblest and most lyrical of all funeral orations – 'And renowned be thy grave'.

5

THE UNBELIEVERS

Most ignorant of what he's most assur'd. – *Measure for Measure* II.ii

We now enter a world of vain bibble-babble and sheer madness. It is known variously as the Baconian Heresy, the Baconian Controversy, Anti-Stratford or the Shakespeare Claimants (for their name is legion – they are many). The starting point of its well-meaning amateur supporters – for in this strange world they are all honourable men – is the 'fact' that Will Shagsper, a Warwickshire clod and unlettered oaf who never (dammit!) went to a university, was clearly quite incapable of writing the plays and poems so wrongly attributed to him.

This quaint nonsense is a compound of ignorance, total incomprehension of the nature of creative writing, let alone the mystery of genius, and the most nauseating snobbery. It officially began in the eighteenth century when a Herbert Lawrence first publicly doubted Shakespeare, but it did not get under way until the mid-nineteenth century. An American named Joseph C. Hart brought the matter up again, then W. H. Smith put up the idea that Bacon was the author.

At this point an American lady named Delia Bacon (!) laid into the Stratford poacher and his 'dirty, doggish group of players' – they included at least two church-wardens, Heminge and Condell – and publicly announced (in 1857) that an illiterate country bumpkin could never have written the immortal works. The good lady naturally knew nothing of Shakespeare's family and Elizabethan Stratford. Few then did. (Few of today's anti-Stratfordians do either, and their crime is far greater than poor Delia Bacon's.)

After Miss Bacon, cypher-crazed experts got to work, culminating in the sensational 'discovery' of the American ex-Senator of Minnesota, Ignatius Donnelly. In his *The Great Cryptogram* (1888) he revealed the hidden message of the First Folio, that Bacon not only wrote Shakespeare but Marlowe, Montaigne, and Burton's *The Anatomy of Melancholy* as well. Mark Twain joined the ranks, and other Baconians included such Shakespearean scholars as Count Bismarck and Sigmund Freud (who, incidentally, believed that Cordelia was the embodiment of the death wish).

Then came a true sensation. Sir Edward Dunning in *Bacon is Shakespeare* (1911) found that the word 'Honorificabilitudinitatibus' in *Love's Labour's Lost* V.i.44 meant HI LUDI F. BACON NATI TUITI ORBI – 'these plays, offspring of F. Bacon, are preserved for the world'. No prizes are offered for whatever else can be got from the word. By such methods it is possible to prove that Bernard Shaw wrote the plays, or that the peasant Verdi was a front man for some scholarly Italian duke.

Then came embarrassing divisions in the anti-Stratford ranks. Heresy broke out among the heretics. The claims of the Earls of Oxford, Rutland, Southampton and Derby were canvassed, along with others, including Gloriana herself. Some believed that a consortium wrote the works – what a giant conspiracy that would have been! Of course, few of the main contenders – there are over fifty claimants – are known to have written a line of blank verse, but what of that? The lunacy culminated very happily when J. Freeman Clarke announced that Shakespeare wrote Bacon.

There was some excuse (though not much) for the early anti-Stratford men and women, because, as we have seen, they knew little of Shakespeare's family and his home town, not even that his parents were middle-class. Not that a child of 'bumpkins' could not be a genius. But then the world of anti-Shakespeare is divided into lords and bumpkins with few in between, or so it would seem.

The only heresy which deserves more than an amused glance is the Marlovian one, and it should be stressed that the only reason for giving space to anti-Stratford at all is because the chasers after phantoms who indulge in it have had, and still have, much publicity.

Disciples of the Marlovian cult, as was briefly mentioned in Chapter 2, believe that Christopher Marlowe, undead, wrote Shakespeare's plays, having survived his tavern brawl. Kit Marlowe at least was a genius, but supporters of his claims know remarkably little of his works. The brazen splendour of his world, an epic world on occasion, is peopled by characters who are rarely humorous and equally rarely more than two-dimensional. It is leagues away from 'gentle' Shakespeare's boundless humanity and infinite variety. Shakespeare even mocked his admired forerunner on occasion, notably with Pistol. A mere glance at *The Jew of Malta* and Shylock should be enough to show the difference between the two men and their art, and early Shakespeare, though by no means as good as Marlowe at his grandest and most poetic, already shows signs of outstripping his rival in *Henry VI* and *Richard III*, just as the young, crude Verdi instantly proclaimed himself likely to overtake the more refined man-of-the-moment, Donizetti.

It must be stated frankly, however, that though no reputable scholar in this century has ever doubted Shakespeare's authorship, it cannot be proved that he wrote the plays. Playwrights were not news in those days, there were no newspapers, obvious enough points perhaps, but in the business of exploding the pretentious twaddle of the anti-Stratford camp the obvious has to be stated.

But there are many reasons for belief, common sense apart, and many ways of demolishing the 'proofs' of the opposition. Most notably, there is the sheer absurdity of the suggestion that Shakespeare's close friends were all part of a giant plot to keep a most extraordinary secret safe; in fact, that they were knaves, for living so closely together for so long they could hardly not know. The most significant and clinching opinion is that of his friend, rival and critic on occasion, Ben Jonson. If anyone can believe that Jonson's *De Shakespeare Nostrati*, loving and critical, is a fraud – for Jonson would certainly have known the truth – let him roast in the mines of sulphur, or, better still, stick to reading the less demanding type of whodunnit.

But where, asks the Baconian, did Shagsper get his great knowledge? If such a person picks up this book he will possibly turn to this chapter first, whereas in Chapter 2, as other readers will have noted, Shakespeare's education and the nature of creative writing are discussed. Of course, Shakespeare must have been prepared to accept advice from all sorts of men and women, even Sir Francis Bacon. Why not?

Perhaps treatment for an anti-Stratfordian should include regular visits to an Irish pub: there are plenty in Britain. It may gradually dawn on him that mere learning does not make a man use words like a god. The Irish are glorious talkers, but the Elizabethans, word-drunk and with their language in a ferment, must have been stupendous at the intoxicating game.

Actors know instinctively that Shakespeare the writer and Shakespeare the actor were one. As for the scholarly attitude, it has never been summed up better than by F. E. Halliday in his essential A to Z of Shakespeareana, *A Shakespeare Companion*. He remarks how Baconians still base their 'crazy structures' on nineteenth-century scholarship, but adds that it would be a pity if their magazines stopped publishing their entertaining fantasies. How tolerant Professor Halliday is. Less kindly critics might suggest that Baconians and the rest inform themselves of the evidence we do possess, learn about Tudor London and the fine little town of Stratford, even read Bacon, or, better still, try reading the plays for sheer joy.

6

NOT JUST AN INDUSTRY - MORE A WAY OF LIFE

For the lad of all lads was a Warwickshire lad. – David Garrick, 1769
The play's the thing. – Hamlet II.ii

The traveller on a pilgrimage usually finds what he wants to find. A few tourist attractions – the Grand Canyon, Chartres Cathedral, the Tower of London, the Victoria Falls and other classics of the trade – are guaranteed successes, but most shrines, man-made or otherwise, depend on previous knowledge and love for full effect.

Stratford-upon-Avon, Warwickshire, is no exception. Visitors uninterested in Shakespeare – the percentage is unguessable – must find it pleasant enough, for there are plenty of charming old houses, and the river is sure to raise the bleakest spirits at any time of the year. Yet even some Shakespeare-lovers find the place a little disappointing, for there is nothing so obviously actual, dramatic, evocative and haunting as there is, say, at Haworth, in Yorkshire, the place and the parsonage being so emotion-charged that even a visitor whose only knowledge of the Brontës comes from Hollywood cannot fail to be stirred.

For the lucky ones, Stratford, too, is unique, and some of it, for the happy visitor who has Shakespeare, the theatre and Elizabethan England in his blood, is emotional dynamite.

There are moments when it can seem too good to be true. To visit the Royal Shakespeare Theatre's picture gallery and finish at the display cases overlooking the Avon, to stand looking down in awe at the very scales used by Irving as Shylock in 1880, at his cap as Romeo, at mementoes of Siddons and Ellen Terry, then to raise one's eyes to gaze across a trim lawn to the sweep of the river and to Holy Trinity

Church beyond . . . this is ecstasy or, it must be admitted, merely a way of passing the time, according to taste.

Much of Stratford is like that, with the visitor's feelings colouring everything, though this does less than justice to the Shakespeare Birthplace Trust, whose work in preserving the several Holy Grails of the Shakespeare Industry is as admirable as it is unostentatious. And if there are Gifte Shoppes permutating the Bard into profit, only the over-sensitive can react enough to let it spoil a visit. It is hard to believe that Shakespeare would have resented being turned into an industry.

One feature of the town that is not generally realised is how quiet it mostly is even at the height of the season – which, incidentally, never ends, as January visitors know. Before the reader, well aware that Stratford is one of the busiest small towns on earth, assumes that the author is indulging in the most brazen lies, the quiet must be explained. It is true that Henley Street, with busloads attacking the Birthplace like waves of troops going over the top hour after hour, is a busy little glory-place, but Bridge Street is wide enough to cope with its responsibilities and the Bancroft Gardens absorb their groundlings happily. Head down High Street towards other sacred spots and soon the peace descends: it never leaves some of the centre of the town's side streets. Generally, the impression of a quiet little market town remains, though it has ten times as many people as in Shakespeare's day, and its newer suburbs are anything but Shakespearean.

British Rail ensures that most people approach Stratford by road. Sunday, the key visitors' day, finds the unwary traveller trainless. The trip from Leamington by rail, when one is allowed to make it, is a joy, a bonus being that Wilmcote and other little stations delight even those who cannot usually muster up Betjemanesque feelings.

It is hard to imagine even the most biased supporters of other counties not responding to Warwickshire's charms. Those who cannot understand how Shakespeare could leave London with all its excitements not only fail to appreciate the love of a countryman for his earth, his blessed plot, but also cannot know that Warwickshire, lying at England's heart, is what countless millions believe the English countryside to be.

Though the Royal Shakespeare Theatre is a Midlands theatre, with many regular patrons from the cities and towns to the north of it, along with Shakespeare-lovers from everywhere save the Arctic and

Antarctic, visitors to Stratford are more likely to come by coach, car and train from the south. The road from London via Oxford, after the attractions of Buckinghamshire and Oxfordshire, offers a striking first view of Warwickshire, looking down from a hill on rolling country-side. The champagne mood is increased by passing through Long Compton, which is so exuberantly thatched that it is hard for even the most careful driver to concentrate on his job.

On through country which becomes less hilly, but remains lovely even in wet November, and the traveller comes to Stratford, crossing the Avon over Clopton Bridge, which is even older than Shakespeare.

On his first visit, the tourist's supreme goal must always be the Birthplace in Henley Street, even though it cannot be proved that it was there that was heard 'the first puling cry which announced he was living and healthy', as Benjamin Haydon put it. In Shakespeare's day the building was two separate but adjoining houses, the eastern half being his father's business premises.

The most granite-hearted visitor must surely experience something of the thrill of being 'on the spot' at his first visit, yet this 'fiercely preserved' building, as J. C. Trewin has called it, is not particularly romantic. That is no criticism of the Shakespeare Birthplace Trust, which preserves all its charges with discreet dignity. If the word 'tasteful' had not become debased, it would admirably sum up the Trust's work. The western half of the building is now domestic, the eastern half a museum. The holy of holies, the birth room, drew this comment from Haydon: 'As people are generally born in bedrooms, why this upstairs room probably gave birth to the poet.' Why not indeed?

'An excellent restoration of an Elizabethan house known to have existed in something like its present form when Shakespeare was born' was Christian Deelman's summing-up of the building in *The Great Shakespeare Jubilee*. Unlike Anne Hathaway's Cottage, it seems more house than home, though everything comes to life in the back garden, which is full of flowers, herbs and trees that Shakespeare knew and mentioned in his plays.

More romantic by far is Anne Hathaway's (father's) Cottage a mile away at Shottery, which is now linked to the town. 'Cottage' is a misnomer for a twelve-roomed building, which remained in the Hathaway family until 1892, when the Birthplace Trust took it over.

SHAKSPEARE'S HOUSE,

AT

Stratford-on-Avon.

MR. ROBINS

Feels highly flattered at having been selected by the Representatives of the late Mr. THOMAS COURT, to submit to Public Competition,

AT THE AUCTION MART, LONDON,

On Thursday, 16th of September, 1847,

AT TWELVE O'CLOCK,

THE TRULY

HEART-STIRRING RELIC

OF A MOST GLORIOUS PERSON, AND OF

ENGLAND'S

IMMORTAL BARD

Which, by the course of events, and directions contained in the Will of the late Owner, must be offered to Public Sale; yet with every fervent hope that its appreciation by the Public will secure for it a safeguard and continuance at the Birth and Burial-place of the Poet,

THE MOST HONOURED MONUMENT OF THE GREATEST GENIUS THAT EVER LIVED.

To attempt to paraphrase this interesting and singular Property would be to Vain, we (to Quote his Poetical Sentiment thus),—

To gild refined gold, to paint the lily,
To throw a perfume on the violet,
To smooth the ice, or add another hue
Unto the rainbow, or with taper light
To seek the beauteous eye of Heaven to garnish,
Is wasteful and ridiculous excess.

Mr. ROBINS, therefore, simply invites all those who take an interest in this Monumental Relic (and who is there amongst us does not) to pay a visit to Stratford-on-Avon, in the full assurance that what they will see and find, now that this remarkable Property may be possessed, will raise a spirit of Competitive hitherto unknown. THE

Swan & Maidenhead, a thriving Public House

Which adjoins, with its Out-buildings, forms part of the Property, extending from Henley Street to the Guildpits; the whole of which, be it remembered, is

FREEHOLD.

Much of the furniture belonged to the family, there is plenty to look at for the lover of social history, and the garden is so beautiful that even a hay-fever sufferer can bear it in June. About fifty thousand or so come to the Cottage every year. (My own first visit was one February day of rain and sleet. There were a dozen or so others at that moment in its history, including three Brazilians, four Japanese, two Americans and three Britons, a typical Stratford assortment. There was a loving guide, and the four corners of the earth seemed glad they had come.)

Nearly four miles north of Stratford at Wilmcote is Mary Arden's House – meaning her father Robert's, a fine farmhouse with oak beams from Arden forest, a large dovecote and historic farming implements in buildings at the back. It is the most distant of the Birthplace Trust's charges.

Back in Stratford, Hall's Croft, home of Susanna and her Puritan husband, the fashionable Doctor Hall, is as imposing as its walled garden (a modern re-creation) is beautiful. The Doctor's dispensary is to be seen, complete with apothecaries' jars for herbs, pills and medicines, etc. He wrote *Select Observations on English Bodies or Cures both Empiricall and Historicall, performed upon very eminent Persons in desperate Diseases*. One of his poultices was of 'swallows' nests, dirt, dung and all, boiled in oil of chammumel and lilies, beaten and passed through a sieve'. Other ingredients included 'dog's turd'. The house contains a hall turned lecture and exhibition room, and also the Festival Club's reading-room. The Trust, getting it in 1949, has restored it to its Jacobean splendour.

Susanna and John lived there until Shakespeare's death, when they moved into New Place, the grand house that is lost to us except for its foundations, for it was pulled down in 1677. The pleasant Knott Garden, a replica of an Elizabethan one, is entered through Nash's House, Nash being the first husband of Shakespeare's grand-daughter, Elizabeth Hall. Nash was a good Royalist and once entertained Queen Henrietta Maria at New Place, left him by John Hall. Her husband, Charles I, being a keen Shakespearean, what would we not give for an account of the proceedings by a Pepys or a Boswell?

All the Birthplace Trust properties are open from April to October, while from November to March only the essentials, the Birthplace and Anne Hathaway's Cottage, can be visited.

The Trust's headquarters, the Shakespeare Centre, was opened in 1964 and is run by Dr Levi Fox, who has made it a focal point for Shakespearean scholarship and has himself produced a number of pictorial guides to the Trust's charges and about Shakespeare and Stratford. That the Centre was opened by an American, Eugene Black, is a proper reminder of how much Stratford, both theatre and town, owes to American generosity.

One building in the town is actually owned by an American institution (two, if the reader feels that a Hilton Hotel is an American institution). This is the Harvard House, built by the father-in-law of Robert Harvard, whose son was to found the famous American university, which now owns the house. This was partly due to the popular novelist and keen Stratford citizen, Marie Corelli. She had bought the house to preserve it, then, finding herself amongst millionaires on Sir Thomas Lipton's yacht, persuaded one of them, Edward Morris of Chicago, to buy it. He restored it in 1909 and gave Harvard the title-deeds.

Stratford is too rich in treasures for a short chapter to cover them all, so, noting that Shakespeare's school, Stratford Grammar School, can be visited, but only in the summer holidays, we must conclude the non-theatrical part of our tour at a building which would decidedly justify a visit, even if it had no Shakespearean connections.

This is Holy Trinity Church and, except for its spire, it is the building that Shakespeare knew. Lucky the visitor who first approaches its Valhalla at a quiet moment in a less crowded part of the year, for it is deeply moving to stand gazing down at the five simple gravestones: from left to right they belong to Anne, William, Thomas Nash, Susanna and John Hall. The uninspiring bust looks over them from the left.

> Good frend, for Jesus sake forbeare
> To digg the dust encloased heare.
> Bleste be the man that spares thes stones
> And curs't be he that moves my bones!

So exhorts the wording on Shakespeare's grave. Nobody seems to think that Shakespeare perpetrated the rather haunting doggerel, which was possibly put there to stop a later sexton placing a new grave on the spot and moving his bones to the charnel house, as was the custom.

The curse happily has worked, though some anti-Stratfordians long to play the Resurrection Man in the interests of their ludicrous theories, believing that All will be Revealed if the tomb is desecrated.

Outside the church is sheer beauty, the Avon, the willows, the fields, the sound of the weir combining into a demi-paradise.

Playgoing at Stratford is so logical an activity that it comes as a shock to realise that for two centuries after his death no one could say in excitement, 'The actors are come hither.' In London, as soon as Charles II was restored, Shakespeare was restored also, though, as we have seen, the taste of the day required 'improvements'. But the traditions were guarded, especially of acting, for Betterton and other Restoration actors were able to learn from old players, even if the theatres were now very different.

At Stratford, however, there was a blank. The growing interest in Shakespeare's life and works in the early eighteenth century was not enough to revive the drama in his seemingly remote birthplace. Strolling players broke the long silence in 1746, then, in 1769, came David Garrick's Shakespeare Festival. The great actor, supreme in tragedy and comedy alike, master-minded the Jubilee, a three-day junket which included parades, balls, fireworks, and Garrick himself rendering *Ode upon Dedicating a Building and Erecting a Statue to Shakespeare*. Despite almost continuous rain, everyone seems to have had a grand time when they could amid the floods and in their soggy clothes, and nobody noticed until later that not a single full line of Shakespeare's had been uttered publicly. The nearest to it was 'We ne'er shall look upon his like again!' in the *Ode*, five words of which come from *Hamlet*.

Shakespeare's 300th birthday in 1864 was a good excuse for another (drier) celebration, including six plays, and it was the turning-point in Stratford's theatrical history. That year's mayor was the rich brewer, Edward Fordham Flower, and his son Charles was to prove even more of a friend and patron of the theatre than the rest of his public-spirited descendants. He proposed that a permanent playhouse be built in the 1870s, he gave some land on the Bancroft, the river meadow where Garrick had erected a Rotunda for his Jubilee, and he organised a Shakespeare Memorial Association to build a theatre, a picture gallery and a library, giving more money than anyone else.

While non-Stratfordians sneered at the presumptions of a small

FIRST DAY,

Wednesday, the 6th of SEPTEMBER,

Shakespeare's Jubilee.

The STEWARD of the Jubilee begs Leave to inform the COMPANY, that at Nine o'Clock will be

A PUBLIC BREAKFAST

At the TOWN-HALL:

Thence to proceed to the CHURCH to hear

The ORATORIO of JUDITH,

Which will begin exactly at ELEVEN.

From Church will be a full CHORUS of VOCAL and INSTRUMENTAL MUSIC to the AMPHITHEATRE; where, at Three o'Clock, will be

An ORDINARY for Gentlemen and Ladies.

About Five o'Clock, a Collection of NEW SONGS, BALLADS, ROUNDELAYS, CATCHES, GLEES, &c. will be performed in the AMPHITHEATRE; after which the Company is desired to prepare for the BALL, which will begin exactly at Nine, with NEW MINUETS, (composed for the Occasion) and played by the whole Band.

The SECOND DAY'S ENTERTAINMENTS will be published To-morrow.

N. B. As the PUBLIC BREAKFASTS and ORDINARIES are intended for those Ladies and Gentlemen who have taken the Guinea Tickets, no Person can be admitted without first shewing such Ticket. Should there be Room for more than the Proprietors of those Tickets, Ladies and Gentlemen will be admitted to the ORATORIO and FIREWORKS, at *Five Shillings* each; and to the DEDICATION, ODE, and BALL, at *Half a Guinea* each.

*** The STEWARD hopes that the Admirers of *Shakespeare*, will, upon this Occasion, wear the Favors which are called the *Shakespeare Favors*.

☞ As many Ladies have complained of the Fatigue they shall undergo, if the Ball and Masquerade are on two successive Nights, there will be only the FIREWORKS on *Thursday* Night, and the MASQUERADE on *Friday* Night, the 8th Inst. which will conclude the Entertainments of the Jubilee.

STRATFORD: Printed by FULK WEALE, next Door to the Coffee-House.

market town, work went ahead. The great day came on 23 April (of course) 1879, when a strange modern Gothic building was opened. Its stage was too shallow, but it was good for actors and audiences because of its intimacy, and it even had one admirer of its architecture, Oscar Wilde, who paid it a visit in the 1880s. *Much Ado* was the first play, starring Helen Faucit and Barry Sullivan, a vigorous actor, whom Bernard Shaw was later to praise at the expense of Irving.

Not until 1886 was there true theatrical continuity at the Memmorial Theatre, as it was then called. That year Frank Benson and his young company took over and played nearly every spring until 1919. Handsome, idealistic and athletic, Benson at his best – Richard II was his most famous part – was a very fine actor. Later his mannerisms were sneered at, as was his alleged mania for sports and sporting actors. The joke has backfired. Like many of today's actors, he believed that his players could give of their best only if they were fit, their bodies supple and responsive. The most famous sporting story was true, if misunderstood. He once sent a young actor a telegram: 'You must play Rugby', meaning the part in *The Merry Wives*, not the game.

By 1910, Benson was giving a spring and a summer season, each a month long. Guest players sometimes joined him for a performance, among them Ellen Terry and Beerbohm Tree, while those he trained included Henry Ainley and what appears on paper to have been a large minority of the Profession of his day. He was knighted at Drury Lane during the Shakespeare Tercentenary Matinee in 1916.

Benson was asked not to act, just manage, in 1919. He refused, and left the Memorial Theatre to others. In 1926 it was burnt to a shell, only the library and gallery surviving. Bernard Shaw sent a message of congratulations, looking forward to a more modern theatre, and hoped that a few other theatres would catch fire. For six years Shakespeare was banished to a cinema, but, meanwhile, funds for another theatre were being raised, Americans being to the fore, and in 1932, the new theatre, designed by Elisabeth Scott, opened on the usual day. Now regarded as a pleasure to behold, it was hailed by some as a factory or a tomb. Audiences steadily rose to 200,000 by 1939, but a chasm divided actors and audiences. Baliol Holloway, a Stratford regular, said it could be like playing to Boulogne from the beach at Folkestone.

Salaries were too small to attract the leading actors of the day, but fine work was done by younger actors like Donald Wolfit, and the veteran Randle Ayrton. In 1944–5 Robert Atkins, once an Old Vic actor and director, and before he became the witty, earthy regular ruler of the Open Air Theatre, Regent's Park, had the action brought forward, but the chasm remained. The theatre's modern history began in 1946, when Sir Barry Jackson of Birmingham Rep fame, took charge, encouraged young talents like Peter Brook and Paul Scofield, and raised standards to the point that no one could sneer 'provincial' at any of the proceedings. From 1948 to 1959, under Anthony Quayle and then Glen Byam Shaw, seasons of great content and occasional glory were given, Gielgud, Olivier, Peggy Ashcroft, Edith Evans and Michael Redgrave being only some of the names who appeared. And the chasm vanished in 1951, the interior being remodelled.

Among the peaks of achievement of those years was that rarest of theatrical occasions, a successful *Antony and Cleopatra*, directed by Byam Shaw and with Michael Redgrave and Peggy Ashcroft (1953); Peter Brook's now legendary resurrection of *Titus Andronicus* with Olivier (1955); Olivier's *Macbeth* in the same season; and Guthrie's *All's Well*, with Edith Evans as the Countess (1959).

That season *Coriolanus*, with Olivier, was directed by Peter Hall. Next year the twenty-nine-year-old master of all theatrical trades was in charge at Stratford, now transformed into the Royal Shakespeare Company. Good as previous seasons had been, and despite London seasons and world tours, there had been none of the continuity of a regular ensemble, which is what Hall, with his co-directors, Michael St Denis and Peter Brook, set out to create.

Their success is now theatre history. With a London base at the Aldwych, and with actors on long-term contracts, but with time off for other assignments, the RSC after a season or two of finding a style, became perhaps the most admired company in the world. The turning-point was *The Wars of the Roses* in 1963. This was the three parts of *Henry VI* turned into two plays by Hall's co-director, John Barton, with *Richard III* added to them. In 1964, all the histories were done to celebrate Shakespeare's 400th birthday, and a style had been created: meaningful (to use a debased word) verse-speaking, swift action and totally functional and unrealistic scenery, highlighted by props and costumes which, whether realistic or timeless, are often made of authentic materials. John Bury set *The Wars of the Roses* in a steel frame with props and furniture of iron to match the harsh story; Brook's *Lear*, with Scofield, was set, as J. C. Trewin has written, in 'a world of leather and rusted metal'. And the trend has continued.

The RSC, stressing ensemble, another word for teamwork, has publicly attacked the star system from time to time, and occasionally and unforgivably cast some parts which demand stars too weakly. Fortunately, this is usually accidental. Its roster is too riddled with stars – Peggy Ashcroft, Judi Dench, Donald Sinden, Brenda Bruce, Richard Pasco and native ones like Elizabeth Spriggs, Ian Richardson, David Warner, Tony Church, Janet Suzman and Susan Fleetwood – for this usually to matter, but it is sheer hypocrisy to pretend that certain great parts can be played by non-stars. They cannot, and there's an end on't.

By 1963, the RSC was playing in all to three-quarters of a million a year; now, with the season in Stratford running from March to December, the number is half a million in Stratford alone. Trevor Nunn, director of the Roman plays in 1972, is Peter Hall's successor, and if the occasional bizarre production occurs – eg *Romeo* 1973 – the standard remains high. The RSC, committed to both Stratford and London, is impatient, exciting and aspiring. It is run by people who care about Shakespeare, who believe that because he is 'for all time' he can be interpreted afresh for every generation. If this sometimes leads to failure and even disaster, it also means that for the actors, directors and designers, and therefore the audiences, Shakespeare lives. In the best sense of the word Stratford is a Shakespeare workshop. In the same season, 1973, as the very controversial, in parts sick, *Romeo*, was seen a bolder, far more truthful *Richard II*. It was directed by John Barton, with Richard Pasco and Ian Richardson alternating between Richard and Bolingbroke, and with Tony Church speaking 'This royal throne of kings' as if newly minted.

In 1972, the inside of the theatre was altered yet again, making the stage almost a living thing, so versatile are its movements up and down. It is now as far forward as the old chasm was backward, while live music, as befits a subsidised theatre, is continually i' the air, or rather, with brass so often in the ascendant, we can say with Pistol, 'There roar'd the sea, and trumpet-clangor sounds.'

No visitor with the slightest interest in theatre history should miss the picture gallery and museum beside the theatre. Portraits abound and, as mentioned earlier, there are some moving mementoes.

So our brief tour of the Shakespeare Industry in Stratford ends, as it should, in the theatre. It could end in a dozen happy inns, some of which are historic, but perhaps it should close as one leaves a performance and wanders down to gaze at the moonlit river, and to think about the man from Warwickshire who is the central figure in the culture of the English-speaking world and who reigns far beyond it.

There are two other Stratfords, both of which have honourably turned themselves into focal points of the Industry. The more important one is Stratford, Ontario, whose Shakespearean Festival was the brainchild of a local journalist named Tom Patterson. Inspired during World War II by Italian opera, then by the classical theatre he saw in London, he managed to convince his local authorities that an annual Shakespeare season was possible. They sent him to England to consult that fount of theatrical excitement and daring, Tyrone Guthrie, and a year later the Festival was under way in a large tent with challenging open stage and with Guthrie in charge.

The first play was *Richard III* with Alec Guinness as the lump of foul deformity, elvish-mark'd, abortive rooting hog, and supported by an Anglo-Canadian cast. Casts have become splendidly Canadian down the years, though English guests including Paul Scofield, Alan Bates, and Irene Worth, and Americans like Jason Robards Jnr and Julie Harris have appeared. The native stars include Christopher Plummer, John Colicos, William Hutt and Douglas Rain. The permanent theatre dates from 1957, and its design inspired Chichester's. Non-Shakespearean plays are also given, and the theatre ranks as perhaps the most influential in North America.

The American Shakespeare Festival at Stratford, Connecticut, has flourished since 1955, being largely the creation of Lawrence Langer. Its lack of a distinctive style has been criticised down the years, but it does fine work, including touring, and occasionally provides magnificent performances, most notably the Lear of Morris Carnovsky. Katherine Hepburn and Alfred Drake played Beatrice and Benedick there.

Despite the dearth of public theatres (as opposed to university ones) in the USA, Shakespeare surfaces in many places. He is given free in Central Park, New York, the master of ceremonies being Joseph Papp, now a man of great influence in the city's theatrical life. There are Shakespeare festivals in Oregon, Ravinia, Illinois and elsewhere, and the plays are given in many cities and universities including at the Tyrone Guthrie, Minneapolis: Guthrie enjoyed founding theatres and running them as much as he loved directing and actors loved working for him.

These happenings are encouraging, for Shakespeare had a great tradition in America from the eighteenth century until between the wars. Needless to say, things were tricky in New England, home of Puritanism, for many years. The Sheriff of Boston put paid to a theatre season in 1792, which included *Hamlet* and *Richard III*. This was bad luck on the citizens who had at least been able to see some plays during the British occupation, the Redcoats not having bothered about local edicts forbidding such wicked activities.

The nineteenth century was the grandest time for Shakespeare in America, with visiting stars like Edmund Kean, Macready and Irving, and magnificent American Shakespeareans, culminating in Edwin Booth. It was his crazed brother, John Wilkes Booth, who murdered a keen Shakespeare-lover, Abraham Lincoln. There have been great visitors in our time, but all too few major American Shakespeareans since John Barrymore's day. Shakespearean scholarship, however, is as much an American as a British industry, and the Folger Shakespeare Library, the inspiration of the collector, Henry Folger (1857–1930), is a matchless institution, set in Washington, and housing, amongst other treasures, no fewer than seventy-nine First Folios!

Shakespeare had to await the Romantic age to gain a real foothold in France, for in Voltaire's day he seemed a barbarian, ie did not obey the classical models so admired by the French. Victor Hugo was one of his greatest champions, and Berlioz was another, not merely because he fell violently in love with a visiting Shakespearean actress, Harriet Smithson. Today Shakespeare is often performed at festivals and in Paris and elsewhere.

His reputation has always been higher in Germany, where he has been blessed with more than one excellent translator, and where he is now more performed than Schiller. A century ago he was inspiring actors, designers and directors to experiment. Today, along with often fine acting and staging, goes political controversy, with East and West not sharing the same views of the more political plays. Shakespeare lives indeed in Germany.

Italy, though a number of plays are set there, did not really discover Shakespeare until the nineteenth century. The most famous Italian Shakespearean has been Verdi, who even pulled off the unique feat of matching one of the great tragedies in his *Otello*, with its suberb libretto by the poet and composer, Boito. Duse, Italy's greatest actress, was Boito's lover for a time. Though she played Juliet at fourteen, she is not primarily remembered as a Shakespearean, unlike her fellow Italian, Salvini, whose Othello, noble, volcanic and tigerish, was acclaimed in Europe, Britain and America.

In nearly every European country Shakespeare now flourishes, in none more so than in Russia. True, after the Revolution fatuous attacks were made on him, some questioning his right to survive in a classless society which required only classless literature, but all such nonsense is now forgotten. Tolstoy's attacks on his fellow genius, however, are not, for they are good fun, though meant as the very opposite. We learn that *Julius Caesar* is 'amazingly foul. If I were young and healthy, I'd write an article about it. To rid people of the necessity of pretending that they like it'. Artists can be the best or the worst judges of other artists, but some of Tolstoy's remarks sound like sour grapes at another's reputation, even though he confessed himself prejudiced against the 'insignificant and immoral works' of the poet. It cannot have helped that other great Russians lauded Shakespeare and that Pushkin was one of those who was influenced by him, notably in *Boris Godunov* and *Angelo*.

A genius that can bestride oceans gradually breaks down all barriers of ideology and even rampant nationalism. In India, where, half a century ago, with national feeling growing fast, he had become an alien to many, interest in Shakespeare is on the increase, not least because of the new translations. The most popular play is apparently *Othello*, regarded by the Indians not surprisingly as a tragedy of caste.

The cinema has helped, though the language barrier is an obstacle in English-speaking countries. Also, producers are very timid about plugging the playwright's name which often fails to get on to posters. The Shakespeare film industry is far bigger than is generally realised. A surprising number of brief films were made in silent days, including a three-minute glimpse of Sarah Bernhardt as Hamlet (1900). (On stage she used to kick Polonius's shins and knock Rosencrantz's and Guildenstern's heads together, events not captured by a camera.) A 1907 *Hamlet* polished off the play in ten minutes flat.

No Anglo-American film has been completely successful, though some are astonishingly valuable as records: the Olivier *Othello*, as performed at the National and later screened; the Mankiewicz *Julius Caesar*, full of fine moments, and capturing Gielgud's Cassius for ever. Olivier's *Henry V* is most people's favourite, and with reason, not least because of its magical evocation of the Globe at the beginning. In the title-role, Olivier played the part as written, not a fashionable thing to do now when patriotism, Elizabethan-style, is trendily out, but dead right for the 1940s. His *Richard III* is a fine film, very strongly cast, even though his own incomparable performance was far more right on the stage. His *Hamlet* won an Oscar, though it was much criticised. Yet in giving a straightforward 'man who could not make up his mind' interpretation, he made it certain that the average cinema-goer would follow the story, which was his duty in a cinema context. A famous foreign Hamlet has been Innokenti Smoktunovsky in a Russian film (1964).

For a full-scale study of this subject, the reader should obtain Roger Manvell's *Shakespeare on Film*, so with apologies to a host of honest and dishonest efforts, some of which made some money, many of which were financial and/or artistic disasters, this section must end with two examples of an ever-hopeful genre.

The first, Reinhardt's *A Midsummer Night's Dream* (1935), lost money and was over-elaborate to a degree. Yet despite miscasting on a monumental scale, it has moments that are superb, like the first sight of Mickey Rooney as a little Puck definitely not of this world, and much of the playing of the Mechanicals, led by James Cagney as Bottom. It ranks as one of the best good-bad films ever made.

The other is the least-known of Orson Welles's Shakespearean films, *Chimes at Midnight* (1966), both parts of *Henry IV* and some of *Henry V* being cleverly compressed into one. Though Welles played Falstaff, he by no means orientated the film to the character, certainly little more than in the plays themselves. Of the famous parts only Glendower is missing. Welles directed the proceedings at a tremendous pace, but with true feeling. A number of the players gave him fine performances, including Gielgud as Henry IV, and the battle of Shrewsbury is one of the best film battles ever. It looks as if it was fought in Spain (where the film was made) rather than Shropshire, but that need worry no one. Few would dare claim that the film is perfect, but Welles and his team created a work of art – nearly every shot is perfection – which is also truly Shakespearean. Everyone knows that *Citizen Kane* is a masterpiece. Everyone should know that this film is, too. Shakespeare-lovers should cross continents to find it.

Artists, other writers, musicians and choreographers have been inspired by Shakespeare to create too many works of art to be listed here. The Shakespeare Industry knows no artistic bounds. But to end we must return to Britain and, especially, to the Old Vic. Whatever the fluctuations of Shakespeare's reputation in his own land, discussed in Chapter 4, it was a line of great and fine actors who, along with receptive audiences, kept Shakespeare alive even when the theatre itself was in a most dismal state. After Burbage, the giants were Betterton, Garrick, Siddons, Kean, Macready (when the theatre was at a very low ebb) and Irving.

There were many others, not least those who took plays to every part of the kingdom. It is beside the point that some of these immortals used flawed texts: they kept Shakespeare alive. After Irving came other famous names, including Tree, Forbes Robertson (an incomparable Hamlet), and Lewis Waller. Irving's leading lady, Ellen Terry, was the best-loved and, more importantly, perhaps the best Shakespearean actress of her day.

Then came World War I, and Shakespeare, indeed all serious theatre, suffered a severe setback. Exactly the opposite occurred in World War II.

He was principally saved by an invincible, earthy, ill-educated, God-intoxicated, anecdote-provoking, glorious woman, Lilian Baylis. True, others helped save him in the war and during the 1920s, most notably Sir Barry Jackson at the Birmingham Rep, but it was Lilian Baylis who was the key figure.

This phenomenon was directly responsible for creating three national theatres, the Old Vic, Sadler's Wells Opera and Sadlers Wells, later the Royal Ballet. She first assisted her aunt, Emma Cons, in managing the Old Vic, then in 1914 she took control and never lost it until she died in 1937. Soon she was presenting Shakespeare and opera in English at popular prices and, at a time when the West End was given over almost entirely to frivolity and the safest of commercial plays, she kept Shakespeare and great drama alive and enabled the *idea* of great acting to survive in London. By the end of the 1920s, with directors of the calibre of Ben Greet, Robert Atkins and Harcourt Williams, the Old Vic's fame was established. By the time she died, with her beloved theatre still unsubsidised yet world-famous, the tide had turned and classical drama had been saved.

Among the key names of the 1930s, few did more for the Vic than Tyrone Guthrie. Such was the prestige of the theatre that Miss Baylis, who reopened Sadler's Wells in 1931, could get the most astonishing range of actors to work for her for very low salaries. She prayed for 'good actors and cheap' because that was all that she could afford. Some of those who played for her were the Thorndikes, Russell and Sybil, John Gielgud, Peggy Ashcroft, Edith Evans, Ralph Richardson and Laurence Olivier. Gielgud, his fame established, was able to branch out into classical management, and his popularity helped re-establish Shakespeare in the West End. Another Old Vic – and Stratford – player, Donald Wolfit, set up a company which brought Shakespeare to the masses all over the country. Its standards varied, its importance did not.

All these strands came together in London during World War II. The Old Vic, bombed in 1940, transferred to the New when it was not touring, and the mid-1940s saw a veritable paradise of Shakespeare and the classics in London, with Gielgud giving *Hamlet*, *Love for Love*, *The Circle* and *The Duchess of Malfi* at the Haymarket, Wolfit becoming the supreme Lear of the century one misty April night in 1944 at the Scala Theatre, and the Old Vic, led by Olivier, Richardson and John Burrell, embarking in 1944 on seasons of such glory that they have not passed into history but into immortality. From those seasons, and mentioning only Shakespearean performances, came two unsurpassed performances of great roles, Richardson's Falstaff and Olivier's Richard

III, while in the great secondary role of Hotspur Olivier was surely the most remarkable Henry Percy since the Hotspur of history.

During the war the longed-for state subsidies began in a small way, and today, especially with ever-rising costs, they are not only far bigger, but more vital than ever. The Shakespeare Industry is now state-subsidised in reps as well as at the Royal Shakespeare Theatre, the National, the Actors' Company, founded by Ian McKellen in 1972, and elsewhere. You may find plenty of him every summer in Regent's Park, where for so long Robert Atkins reigned, and you can catch him sometimes at the Mermaid, but very rarely in the commercial theatre which can no longer afford to stage him to rival the great companies. The National Theatre (about to move at the time of writing to its own home after a decade at the Old Vic) opened in 1963 with *Hamlet* – what else? – and has done occasional Shakespeare since. It is not its primary function, though this has not prevented Olivier's Othello and Shylock being seen and heard in the context of a fine ensemble, with the great actor crowning his Shakespearean career in the former role, and astonishing his admirers as always in the latter. And an all-male *As You Like It*, directed by Clifford Williams, was another major occasion.

Inevitably, a chapter like this must be a thing of shreds and patches to enthusiasts for Shakespearean theatre history, who rightly would like a million words on the subject, so perhaps the way to end a mere few thousand should be to describe the Shakespearean season in London at the time of writing in 1973 – a time of the Roman plays, seen at Stratford in 1972, and now being given at the Aldwych. A highlight is *Antony and Cleopatra*, with Janet Suzman and Richard Johnson as the matchless lovers. Meanwhile, on Bankside, at Sam Wanamaker's admirable Globe theatre, the same play is being given in such a way that the laws of libel prevent frankness, unless one is an invited critic. A rousing musical made from *The Two Gentlemen of Verona* is at the Phoenix, direct from New York. *As You Like It* is in Regent's Park. A male brothel will shortly arrive at the Roundhouse from the Edinburgh Festival, in which frame *Pericles* will be enjoyably presented. London, 1973; and Shakespeare is 409 years old. Shakespeare lives – and somehow survives everything that is done to him.

DATES AND SOURCES

THE COMEDY OF ERRORS

Date Between 1590 and 1594. First recorded performance at Gray's Inn, 28 December 1594.

Sources Principal source was Plautus's *Menaechmi*, with some incidents added from his *Amphitruo*, including the scene where Adriana feasts a man she believes is her husband, who is actually locked out.

TITUS ANDRONICUS

Date Between 1589 and 1594, when its earliest recorded performance took place.

Sources Shakespeare may have revised another's earlier play in 1594. It is now generally accepted that the play we have is wholely or partly his. The original sources are classical. Seneca's *Thyestes* provided the cannibalism, his *Troades*, the Act I sacrifice. Ovid's *Metamorphoses* provided the method by which the raped and mutilated Lavinia could reveal the name of her attackers (the tale of Philomela and Procne). The murderous Moor and a Moor marrying a white (Aaron and Tamora) were common themes.

HENRY VI PART I

Date c1589–90. It may be the *Harey the vj* mentioned by Henslowe in his diary in 1592, given by Lord Strange's Men.

Sources Halle's *The Union of the Two Noble and Illustre famelies of Lancastre and York* and (for the portrait of Joan of Arc) Holinshed's *Chronicles of England, Scotland and Ireland* (1587 ed). Shakespeare's many inventions include the famous rose-plucking scene in the Temple Garden.

HENRY VI PART 2

Date 1590–1. It must have been written before September 1592, when Greene's famous attack on Shakespeare, including a parody of a line from Part 3 (see page 39), appeared.

Sources Holinshed and Halle. Minor sources include More's *Dialogue of the Worship of Images* for Simpcox's false miracle (Act II.i).

HENRY VI PART 3

Date Before September 1592 for the reason mentioned above, presumably between 1590 and 1592.

Sources Holinshed and Halle.

RICHARD III

Date c1592–3. There is no reason to suppose that it did not follow immediately after the three *Henry VI* plays.

Sources Holinshed and Halle, who based their accounts on Polydore Vergil's *Anglicae Historiae* and Sir Thomas More's *History of Richard III*. The Tudor version of Richard's earlier career has rightly been dubbed propaganda but, *pace* the Richard III fan club, few serious historians suggest that he was guiltless of the killing of the princes. No letters please.

THE TAMING OF THE SHREW

Date c1593. In June 1594 the Lord Chamberlain's Men were playing at Henslowe's Newington Butts theatre and gave 'the tamynge of A shrowe' which was probably Shakespeare's play, and not the anonymous *Shrew* of 1589.

Sources The anonymous play mentioned above, and George Gascoigne's *Supposes* for the Bianca sub-plot. This in turn was taken from Ariosto's *I Suppositi*. But the main 'shrewish' theme was a widely popular one.

THE TWO GENTLEMEN OF VERONA

Date 1590–5, probably early in that period rather than later because it is clearly an early work.

Sources The main source was *La Diana Enamorada*, a Spanish prose romance by Jorge de Montemayor (c1521–61), translated into English in 1582.

VENUS AND ADONIS

Date 1592–3 is the probable date, when the plague closed the theatres. It was published in 1593.

Sources The main source was Ovid's *Metamorphoses*, which Shakespeare must have studied at school and knew also in a 1567 translation by Arthur Golding.

THE RAPE OF LUCRECE

Date Between April 1593 and May 1594, on the assumption that the poem is the 'graver labour' mentioned in the dedication to *Venus and Adonis*, which was registered in April 1593.

Sources The primary source was Ovid's *Fasti*, and Shakespeare may also have used Livy, Chaucer and others.

THE SONNETS

Date This has been discussed in Chapter 2 (see page 40).

Sources Usually regarded as personal; those who think otherwise cite Petrarch as their inspiration (in translations), also Samuel Daniel's *Delia*. Ovid was among the influences, but, especially since Rowse's latest theories, it is becoming well-nigh impossible to believe that the poems are not autobiographical.

LOVE'S LABOUR'S LOST

Date *c*1594 because of similarities with the poems.

Sources Shakespeare appears to have invented the plot, despite topical allusions in the play, notably Henry of Navarre's 'little Academe', which included the Duc de Biron (Berowne) and de Longueville (Longaville), both supporters of Henry in his fight for the crown. Navarre's 'Academe' was similar to philosophical debating societies which sprang up in France and Italy. The low characters may have been inspired by the types in the Italian *commedia dell' arte* comedies, as well as by people Shakespeare knew in Warwickshire.

KING JOHN

Date *c*1595–7, though some date it earlier. If Constance's grief over the death of Arthur reflects Shakespeare's over the death of Hamnet the later date is right, for Hamnet died in 1596.

Sources The main source was the anonymous *The Troublesome Raigne of John King of England*, published in 1591, which, if Shakespeare did follow it, he also entirely rewrote: for instance, the earlier play is very anti-Catholic.

RICHARD II

Date 1595–6. A performance which Sir Robert Cecil saw in 1595 of *King Richard* may be *Richard III*. It was registered in 1597.
Sources Holinshed and, assuming the play was written in or after 1595, Daniel's *Civil Wars* (1594). There were also minor sources, while the scene between the Queen and the Gardener was Shakespeare's invention.

ROMEO AND JULIET

Date 1595–6, or possibly earlier, depending how topical allusions are interpreted.
Sources The Tragicall Historye of Romeus and Iuliet (1562). by Arthur Brooke, whose poem was inspired by the French translation of an Italian story. The theme of the lovers was a popular one in Renaissance Italy.

A MIDSUMMER NIGHT'S DREAM

Date 1595–6, based on topical allusions, including Titania's Act II comments on what could be the windy, rainy weather of 1594.
Sources The plot is Shakespeare's. Pyramus and Thisbe came from Ovid, while Chaucer's *The Knight's Tale* would have provided information about Theseus and Hippolyta. Oberon as the Fairy King first appeared in English drama in Greene's *James IV*; Puck goes back to Anglo-Saxon times; and Robin Goodfellow, his other name, had appeared in Scot's *Discoverie of Witchcraft* (1584). Local Stratford lore must have provided much inspiration, too.

THE MERCHANT OF VENICE

Date 1596–8, the line 'And see my wealthy Andrew dock'd in sand' possibly referring to the Spanish *St Andrew*, captured on the Cadiz expedition, news of which reached England in July 1596. Francis Meres mentioned the play in 1598.

Sources There were several. Ser Giovanni Fiorentino's *Il Pecorone* (The Simpleton), printed in 1558, provided the Bond theme; the Casket theme came from Richard Robinson's 1577 version of the fifteenth-century *Gesta Romanorum*; a missing play called *The Jew* seems to have combined both themes; Marlowe's *The Jew of Malta* may have had some influence; and the Jewish-Portuguese Dr Roderigo Lopez was hanged, drawn and quartered in 1594 for allegedly trying to poison the Queen, an event which may have suggested a drama about a villainous Jew.

HENRY IV PARTS 1 AND 2

Date c1597. Meres mentions Part 1 in 1598 and may also mean Part 2 as well, which clearly followed it closely.

Sources Holinshed and Daniel. Hal's riotous youth had already been dramatised in *The Famous Victories of Henry V*, anonymously registered in 1594. In the play Shakespeare found Sir John Oldcastle, the original name of his Falstaff, until Oldcastle's descendants complained. Shakespeare then changed the name, using Sir John Fastolfe as his inspiration. The real Fastolfe had an unjustified reputation as a coward – he appears as one in *Henry VI* – and, interestingly, had a Bardolph in his service, owned a Boar's Head Tavern and had been in the Duke of Norfolk's service! Other, lesser sources were used, but Falstaff's adventures were born in Shakespeare's imagination.

THE MERRY WIVES OF WINDSOR

Date 1597, if recent scholarship linking its first performance with the new Knights of the Garter ceremony that year is correct. One of the Knights was Lord Hunsdon, patron of Shakespeare's company, and the play is full of allusions to Windsor and the Garter.

Sources The plot is probably Shakespeare's, despite occasional topical allusions, including ones about a much-mocked Count of Mömpelgart, who longed to be given the Garter and finally got it. Some claim that, because of the speed at which Shakespeare must have worked after his alleged royal command from Elizabeth to show Falstaff in love, he remade an old play. This supposes Shakespeare could not come up with a play in three weeks; tradition suggests he had only a fortnight. Who dares state flatly that a new play in two weeks was beyond him?

HENRY V

Date 1599, from the reference to Essex's departure for Ireland in the Act V Prologue.

Sources Holinshed and *The Famous Victories of Henry the Fifth*, or an earlier Henry V play, owned by the Queen's Men, which no longer exists. Pistol is thought to be a parody of Tamburlaine and Fluellen one of Sir Roger Williams, a Welsh professional soldier.

JULIUS CAESAR

Date 1599, when Thomas Platter saw it at a Bankside theatre. Meres does not mention it in 1598.

Sources The principal source was Plutarch's *Lives* of Brutus, Caesar and Antony, translated by North (1579) from the French of Amyot (1559). Shakespeare was more favourable to Caesar than Plutarch, however. Caesar's deafness was the playwright's invention, as was his succumbing to the falling sickness.

MUCH ADO ABOUT NOTHING

Date 1598–9. Kempe, the first Dogberry, left the Chamberlain's Men in 1599, while the play is not mentioned by Meres in 1598.

Sources The Beatrice–Benedick plot is Shakespeare's, though their exchanges may have been partly inspired by passages in Castiglione's *Il Libro del Cortegiano* (1528, translated by Hoby, 1561). The Dogberry–Verges plot is Shakespeare's, too, while the Claudio–Hero plot comes from Bandello's *Novelle* (1554) and other sources.

AS YOU LIKE IT

Date 1599–1600. It was registered in 1600, was not mentioned by Meres (1598) and quotes Marlowe's *Hero and Leander*, which was published in 1598.

Sources The principal source is Lodge's novel, *Rosalynde, or Euphues' golden legacie* (1590). Shakespeare invented Touchstone and Jaques, Audrey, William and Sir Oliver Martext and tightened up Lodge's slow plot, which came from a fourteenth-century poem, *The Tale of Gamelyn*, wrongly ascribed to Chaucer.

TWELFTH NIGHT

Date c1600: there are several allusions to events in 1599, including the return of the *Sophy* from Persia, richly laden. Fabian mentions it in Act II.v.200.
Sources The marvellous sub-plot and its characters are Shakespeare's creations. The main plot stems directly from the story of Apolonius and Silla in Barnabe Riche's *Farewell to Militarie Profession* (1581), which can be traced back to the anonymous *Gli Ingannati* (1531), a Sienese comedy.

ALL'S WELL THAT ENDS WELL

Date c1597 if it is the *Love's Labour's Won* mentioned by Meres in 1598; 1602–3, perhaps, if not, the dates chosen because of the likeness to the other Dark Comedies.
Sources The main source is Boccaccio's tale of *Giglietta di Nerbona* in the *Decameron*, translated by William Painter in *Palace of Pleasure* (1566). Parolles may be based on the adventures of the poet Barnabe Barnes (1571–1609).

TROILUS AND CRESSIDA

Date 1601–2, scholars having found references to contemporary satirical plays in the text.
Sources Chaucer's *Troilus and Criseyde*, Caxton's *The Recuyell of the Historyes of Troye* (for his view of the Greek and Trojan warriors), Chapman's translation of the *Iliad* (for his view of the Greeks), Robert Henryson's *Testament of Cresseid*, a fourteenth-century work (for his portrait of Cressida), and other sources. By Shakespeare's day, the jaundiced view of the public and personal tales which make up the play was widely accepted.

MEASURE FOR MEASURE

Date c1604, when it was first performed, though this has been challenged. A few topical allusions have been found to help the dating problem.

Sources Principally, Shakespeare used George Whetstone's *Promos and Cassandra* (1578), based on an Italian story by Cinthio which, in turn, had some basis in fact. Whetstone's play is full of civic corruption, which Shakespeare changed into bawdy and low comedy, to great effect.

HAMLET

Date c1601, from internal evidence, including slighting remarks on child actors, who were threatening the popularity of the Chamberlain's Men (1599–1601). Gabriel Harvey mentioned the play in a marginal note of a copy of Chaucer, which was published in 1598. Harvey referred to Essex who was (clearly) alive still: he was executed in February 1601, which suggests that the play must have been performed by then.

Sources The immediate source was an earlier *Hamlet*, possibly by Kyd, acted in 1594 and now lost. The story was first given literary form – for it goes back to Norse oral tradition – by the Danish historian, Saxo Grammaticus (1150?–1206?), who put it in his *Historia Danica*.

OTHELLO

Date 1604. It is reasonable to assume this, as the play was performed at court on 1 November 1604, and therefore was probably written and first performed earlier in the year.

Sources The main source was Giraldi Cinthio's *Hecatommithi*, the story of Othello being in a novella in this collection of tales. Shakespeare used much of Cinthio's plot, though Alfiero, the Iago character, has more motive, having been spurned by Disdemona (*sic*). He and the Moor kill her with a sand-filled stocking and her relatives kill the Moor in revenge. Shakespeare made the character of the Moor far finer than the original.

KING LEAR

Date 1605–6. The eclipses referred to by Gloucester in the second scene happened in the autumn of 1605, while the play was alluded to in a children's play of 1606 called *The Fleire*.

Sources The principal source was *King Leir*, an anonymous play with a happy ending, first performed in 1594, while the first writer to tell the Lear story clearly was Geoffrey of Monmouth (d1154). Shakespeare invented Lear's madness and took the Gloucester sub-plot from Sidney's *Arcadia*.

MACBETH

Date 1606, from internal evidence, including a clear reference by the Porter to the trial and execution of Father Garnet, a Gunpowder plotter who tried to plead Equivocation. 'O, come in, equivatator' says the Porter. Its shortness has led some to think that it was written for a court performance, as part of the visit of King Christian of Denmark in 1606.

Sources The main source is Holinshed, though, as Shakespeare was not writing a chronicle, he altered the facts: instead of King Duff being murdered by Donwald, he made Duncan the victim. Donwald had an ambitious wife. Wanting to please King James, Shakespeare not only made the most of the witches, but had them hail Macbeth (in Scene 3) very much as three undergraduates had hailed him in a pageant at Oxford in his honour in 1605. Banquo is an unhistorical character but neither king nor playwright knew that. Shakespeare consulted other sources apart from Holinshed, possibly King James's *Daemonologie* (1597).

ANTONY AND CLEOPATRA

Date 1606–7, a revised version of a play on the subject by Samuel Daniel appearing in 1607 and showing similarities with Shakespeare's. This would suggest 1606 as the better date. It was registered in 1608.

Sources The main source was Plutarch's *Antony* in his *Lives*, in North's translation (1579). Play and Plutarch are often fascinatingly close, notably in Enobarbus's great speech about Cleopatra, where Shakespeare transforms fine descriptive writing into verbal magic. A minor source was 'W.B.'s' translation (1578) of Appian's *Civil Wars*.

TIMON OF ATHENS

Date There is little agreement. Perhaps somewhere between 1605 and 1609.

Sources Plutarch's *Lives* of Antonius and Alcibiades, Lucian's dialogue, *Timon, or the Misanthrope*, and possibly an academic play called *Timon*, anonymously written between 1581 and 1590, but not printed (to complicate matters) until modern times.

CORIOLANUS

Date c1608, partly because of its style, partly from topical references, most notably class conflicts in the North and Midlands in 1607.

Sources The principal source was the second edition of North's translation of Plutarch's *Lives* (1595). Livy may have been used amongst minor sources.

PERICLES

Date c1607. It was entered in the Stationers' Register in 1608, and at some time between 1606 and November 1608 the Venetian Ambassador saw it. Though it appeared in quarto in 1609, it was not included in the First Folio.

Sources The main source is John Gower's retelling – in his *Confessio Amantis* (1385–93) – of an old Latin story, 'Apollonius of Tyre'. Also used was the version of the story in Laurence Twine's *The Patterne of Paynfull Adventures* (1576).

CYMBELINE

Date Probably 1609–10, though there is little evidence. Simon Forman saw it in 1611.

Sources The main source for the semi-legendary king and also Belarius, Guiderius and Arviragus was Holinshed. The wager theme stems from Boccaccio's *Decameron*, the story of Bernabo of Genoa.

THE WINTER'S TALE

Date 1611, because of a reference to a New Year's Day court masque and because Simon Forman saw the play in May.

Sources The main source was Robert Greene's romance, *Pandosto or the Triumph of Time* (1588), later reprinted as *Dorastus and Fawnia*. The statue coming to life is in Ovid's *Metamorphoses*, which Shakespeare read at school, the story being Pygmalion and Galatea. He invented a number of characters, most notably Autolycus.

THE TEMPEST

Date 1611. It was presented at court on 1 November and, presumably, was written in the same year.

Sources There were many, including a number for the opening ship-wreck. These were accounts of the wreck of *The Sea Venture* on the Bermudas in 1609 and there were other reports, including the official *A True Declaration of the Estate of the Colonie in Virginia* (1610), which helped with details of the island as well as the wreck. For the main plot Shakespeare may have read Montaigne's essay *On Cannibals* (1603), and a group of pastoral tragi-comedies played in Italy in the sixteenth century and set by the sea, which had a benevolent magician in some of them. These *commedia dell'arte* improvised plays may have been seen in England, presented by touring Italians, or Shakespeare may have read one or two in published form. Some of their scenarios are certainly very close to the play.

HENRY VIII

Date 1613, just before the ill-fated première at the Globe when a cannon set the theatre alight (see page 48).

Sources Holinshed, also Halle's *The Union of the Two Noble and Illustre Famelies of Lancastre and York* (1548), were the main sources, especially the former. The Cranmer story in Act V comes from Foxe's *Book of Martyrs*.

SOME PERSONAL AND PUBLIC EVENTS

1557 John Shakespeare marries Mary Arden.

1558 Queen Elizabeth I succeeds to the throne.

1564 Births of Shakespeare and Marlowe.

1569 John Shakespeare becomes Bailiff (mayor) of Stratford. Rebellion of the Northern (Catholic) Earls.

1572 Birth of Ben Jonson.

1573 Birth of the Earl of Southampton.

1582 Shakespeare marries Anne Hathaway.

1583 Birth of Susanna Shakespeare.

1585 Births of Hamnet and Judith Shakespeare.

1587 Mary, Queen of Scots, executed. Five companies of players visit Stratford.

1588 The Armada. Marlowe now famous.

1590 Publication of Sidney's *Arcadia* and Spenser's *The Faerie Queen* (1–3).

1592 *Harey the vj* performed by Strange's Men. Greene's attack on Shakespeare. Plague closes London's theatres.

1593 *Venus and Adonis* published. Marlowe killed. Plague again closes theatres.

1594 *Titus Andronicus* performed by Sussex's Men. Publication of *The Rape of Lucrece*. In *Willobie His Avisa* (Anon), Shakespeare is first praised and properly named in print. The Lord Chamberlain's Men formed.

1595 Shakespeare, now a principal member of the above company, paid for performances at Court the previous Christmas.

1596   Essex captures Cadiz. Shakespeare living in Bishopsgate, owning goods worth £5. Death of Hamnet. Shakespeare's father granted coat-of-arms. Shakespeare moves south of the river after a quarrel with an unsavoury JP.

1597   Shakespeare buys New Place, Stratford, for £60.

1598   Irish Rebellion begins. Shakespeare plays a principal part in Jonson's *Every Man in His Humour.*

1599   Building of the Globe. Shakespeare a housekeeper (sharer), holding one-tenth of the shares. Essex and Southampton go to Ireland. Thomas Platter of Basle sees *Julius Caesar* at the Globe.

1601   Friends of Essex ask for a performance of *Richard II.* Essex's rebellion and execution. Death of John Shakespeare.

1602   Shakespeare buys farmland and a cottage. Southampton imprisoned in the Tower (released 1603).

1603   Elizabeth I dies, succeeded by James VI of Scotland. Theatres closed by plague. James makes the Chamberlain's Men the King's Men. First Quarto of *Hamlet.* Last recorded performance by Shakespeare – in Jonson's *Sejanus.*

1604   *Othello* performed at Whitehall. Shakespeare lodging with Christopher Mountjoy.

1605   Gunpowder Plot. Augustine Phillips of the King's Men leaves Shakespeare 30 shillings in gold. Shakespeare spends £440 on Stratford tithes.

1606   *Lear* played before James at Whitehall.

1607   Susanna Shakespeare marries John Hall, a very successful Stratford doctor. *Hamlet* performed aboard the *Dragon* at Sierra Leone. Death of Edmund Shakespeare, actor, and presumably William's brother. Jamestown, Virginia, founded.

1608   Shakespeare's grand-daughter, Elizabeth Hall, born. The Blackfriars Theatre leased for twenty-one years by the King's Men. Death of Shakespeare's mother.

1609   The Sonnets published. The King's Men perform thirteen plays during Christmas at Whitehall.

1611   Simon Forman sees *Cymbeline.* Shakespeare helps pay for a Bill for better highways in Parliament. By this time he may have retired to Stratford.

1612   Shakespeare testifies in a suit against Mountjoy. *The Tempest* and *The Winter's Tale* performed by the King's Men.

1613   Shakespeare buys a house in Blackfriars for £140. The Globe is burnt down during the première of *Henry VIII*. Susanna Hall wins her suit against John Lane for defamation of character (alleged adultery).

1614   Re-opening of the Globe. Big fire at Stratford. Document shows Shakespeare owning about 127 acres.

1616   Judith Shakespeare marries Thomas Quiney, a Stratford vintner. Thomas and Judith excommunicated. Shakespeare revises will. Thomas accused of adultery. Death of Shakespeare.

1622   Shakespeare's grand-daughter Elizabeth marries Thomas Nash.

1623   Death of Anne (Hathaway) Shakespeare. The First Folio published.

FOR FURTHER READING

BIOGRAPHY

Brown, Ivor. *Shakespeare* (1949)
Burgess, Anthony. *Shakespeare* (1970)
Halliday, F. E. *The Life of Shakespeare* (1961)
Murry, John Middleton. *Shakespeare* (1936)
Rowse, A. L. *Shakespeare the Man* (1973)

ENCYCLOPEDIAS

Campbell, O. J., and Quinn, E. G. *The Reader's Encyclopedia of Shakespeare* (1966)
Halliday, F. E. *A Shakespeare Companion* (1952, 1964)

GENERAL

Coghill, Nevill. *Shakespeare's Professional Skills* (1964)
Harrison, G. B. *The Elizabethan Journals, 1591–1603* (1938)
——. *A Jacobean Journal, 1603–1606* (1941)
——. *A Second Jacobean Journal, 1607–1616* (1958)
Hodges, C. Walter. *The Globe Restored* (1953)
Holmes, Martin. *Shakespeare's Public* (1960)
Hotson, Leslie. *Shakespeare's Wooden O* (1959)
Joseph, Stephen. *The Story of the Playhouse in England* (1963)
Kott, Jan. *Shakespeare Our Contemporary* (1964)
Nicoll, Allardyce. *British Drama* (5th ed, 1962)
Spurgeon, Caroline. *Shakespeare's Imagery and What It Tells Us* (1935)
Trewin, J. C. *Portrait of the Shakespeare Country* (1970)
——. *Shakespeare on the English Stage* (1964)
Wickham, Glynne. *Early English Stages, 1300–1660*, 2 vols (1959–63)

INDEX

Page numbers in italic type indicate illustrations

Index

Index

Index